D1471944

Searching the Source of the River

Forgotten Women of the Pentecostal Revival in Britain 1907-1914

Diana Chapman

Foreword by Faith Forster

 **PUSH**   **RIVER**CHURCH

Endorsements

"This is a well written, well researched piece of writing on the role of women in the Pentecostal outpouring and Charismatic Movement in the early twentieth century. Every male reader should take note of what happens when the Spirit comes and godly women get released and empowered."

Gerald Coates, Pioneer. Speaker, Author and Broadcaster

"Di challenges us to heed God's instruction to remember and provides the memories. *'The testimony of Jesus is the spirit of prophecy' (Revelation 19:10)*. This testimony of great and courageous yet often unknown women is a prophetic declaration that is waiting for a generation to take hold of and run with again. For the complete story we will wait until eternity but for now we should be grateful to Di for bringing this research into our current experience with a clear cry for these stories to be the fuel for our journey."

Paul Manwaring, Pastor, Bethel Church, Redding, California, USA

"This book adds another fascinating insight into the origins of British Pentecostalism. Its special strength is its focus upon the significant role of women and the key part they played in the early Pentecostal Movement. The selection of characters makes it a fascinating read... There are many important values to this book. It is written in popular form for a wide range of readers, but it is based on detailed research and background study. It will challenge and envision women of today's Pentecostal and Charismatic churches to play a major role in what God is doing. It is a timely reminder in the centenary year of British Pentecostalism that when God pours out His Spirit both 'sons and daughters will prophesy'.

I shall be recommending this fine book to my students and the churches with which I am involved."

Dr. Richard Massey, Former Principal of Birmingham Christian College

"Within the Anglican Church and other denominations, women leaders often have few role models. Where are the women leading large churches or speaking at conferences? In highlighting a number of women who were significant in the early years of British Pentecostalism, Diana Chapman has done a great service for all women in ministry and leadership positions. There may be few contemporary models, but in 'bringing hidden things to light' she reminds us of the great number of women who ministered in this country and overseas in the early twentieth century. Through their lives we gain new insights into how God can use women to play a full part in extending His Kingdom."

Revd. Rosie Ward, Leadership Development Adviser,
Church Pastoral Aid Society [or CPAS]

"The sacrifice and faith of the women of the early twentieth Century Pentecostal revival in Britain challenges and inspires us today. Di Chapman's authoritative and sensitive account draws on richly mined treasure from the past to illuminate the present."

Karen Low, Senior Leader, Antioch Church, Llanelli
Author 'Carriers of the Fire' The Women of the Welsh Revival

"Informative. Inspirational. IMPORTANT. Priority reading! Would that women in all the nations would take a cue from Di Chapman and write God's women back into their own nation's history. Thank God for Di for so skillfully taking up the task in the UK."

Dr. Susan C. Hyatt, Founding Coordinator Int'l Christian Women's Hall of Fame and History Project, Tulsa, OK. USA. Author 'In the Spirit We're Equal'

"It is astonishing how frequently women have been the ones to break barriers, forge new frontiers and advance the cause of the Gospel in fresh and surprising ways. Courage and tenacity matched only by creativity and grace were the hallmarks of so many of these amazing leaders. Diana has done us all a great service by allowing us to know these individuals better. A clear and insightful story."

Revd. Dr. Martin Robinson, National Director, Together in Mission

"Pentecostalism as a movement of churches and people is rapidly coming of age. Many church movements that share a Pentecostal persuasion are approaching their one hundredth anniversaries. This has lead to a new level of self-critique, some introspection and general optimism about the future. Diana Chapman's book represents an important aspect of this new maturity. The willingness to freshly examine gender roles and face our past with frankness is a key element of maturity. Her book makes a valuable and important contribution to this important process and I thus am very glad to commend it and trust that it has a wide and enthusiastic readership."

Paul Alexander, Principal, Mattersey Hall; Member National Leadership Team, British AOG and Chairperson, EPTA.

"This book brings to life the brave and faith-filled endeavours of Spirit filled women in the 20th century's burgeoning Pentecostal Movement. Read and be inspired!"

Revd. Dr. William K. Kay, Director of the Centre for Pentecostal and Charismatic Studies and Reader in Practical Theology, School of Theology and Religious Studies, University of Wales, Bangor

First published in 2007 by **PUSH Publishing**

PUSH Publishing an enterprise division of
City Gateway, BGTC, Hanbury Street,
London, E1 5HZ
www.pushpublishing.co.uk

**A catalogue record for this book is
available from the British Library**

ISBN-10:   0-9553783-1-1
ISBN-13:   978-0-9553783-1-7

Cover design by **Gateway Media**
Typeset by **PUSH Publishing**
Printed and bound in Great Britain
by **T J International Ltd.**, Padstow

Contents

Acknowledgements

We are greatly indebted to Desmond Cartwright for kindly allowing us to reproduce photographs of Margaret Cantel (p.43) and Lydia Walshaw (p.53) and to Tony Cauchi for kindly allowing us to reproduce the picture of Mary Boddy (p.24).

Pictures of *Confidence* magazine covers (p.99), Eleanor Crisp (p.114, *Confidence*, May 1914), and the 'Missionary Ladies' Betty Jones and Grace Elkington (p.132, *Confidence*, Dec 1913) all come from the digitised version of *Confidence* magazine 1908-1926 courtesy of the Revival Library (www.revival-library.org).

The picture of Leith Docks c1920 (p.84) was kindly supplied by John Arthur (www.leithhistory.co.uk). The picture of Carrie Judd Montgomery (p.66) was obtained from the Flower Pentecostal Heritage Centre. Images of 14 Akerman Road, London (p.14), Polly Wigglesworth (p.152) and all other illustrations are courtesy of Joseph Laycock, Gateway Media.

Foreword

Some years ago I heard a preacher telling the inspiring story of Adoniram Judson and his missionary accomplishments in Burma in the early nineteenth century. No mention was made of his wife, but as I listened I began to idly wonder where she (if she existed) figured in this story of heroism and sacrifice. A few years later I came across a short biography of Nancy Judson. I had heard already of Judson's sufferings when thrown into prison, but what was new to me was the story of his wife's courage and faithfulness in visiting the prison daily with her new-born child bringing what scarce food she had, seeking help and release for her husband and ministering the love of Jesus to all she encountered (she was called 'the angel of the prison' by inmates). Shortly after Judson's release from prison she succumbed to a tropical infection and died alone while he was away on missionary work. As I read the account of this beautiful woman's life, I wanted to cry aloud "Thank you, Lord Jesus! Truly this was a woman of God!"

Similar stirrings gripped me as I was reading some of the stories in these chapters. The lives and labours of some of the anointed women of the early 20th century are recorded here. It is a delight to commend this book to you as an inspirational read arising out of solid and painstaking historical research. Covering the history of the Pentecostal Movement as it arose in Great Britain, it particularly charts the contribution of the women leaders. It is notable that when, in the history of God's workings through His Church a new wave of the Spirit arises with fresh understanding, breaking new ground in spiritual life and experience, this is followed by a phase of consolidation where the work is established and structures are put in place to strengthen and stabilise the movement. Sadly, this latter phase is often succeeded by an institutional one when the emphasis is more on the wineskin than on the wine it was once created to contain (and which by now has probably completely evaporated!).

When the Pentecostal move of God began to spread in the UK at the beginning of the 20th century, women as well as men were caught up in its power. A number of women became recognised leaders in the movement, preaching, praying, healing the sick, serving the poor and releasing the power and inspiration of God's Spirit. This is not surprising since women often excel at inspirational leadership, particularly if, as many have, they also possess the gifts to establish and ground the work of God. It is a simple fact that the more institutionalised the Church becomes, the more likely it is to be led by men, with often even the memory or record of women's involvement in the formative stages being erased.

A book like this is refreshing, therefore, in that it redresses the balance somewhat, and in the process provides inspiration and role models for a whole new generation of women as well as men.

The great thing about these stories is that they feature ordinary women – feminine women! – caught up in an extraordinary move of God's Spirit, and being propelled by Him into the forefront of the Pentecostal Movement. They did not lose their godliness or submission to God, and certainly not their down to earth pragmatism, in the process! Rather, they radiate energy, life and love and shine like beacons in the dark for those of us who follow in their footsteps.

I was moved afresh to spiritual hunger as I read of Catherine Price (ch.2), fervently seeking the presence of God in the small hours of the morning in January 1907 and receiving her personal Pentecost as the New Year dawned. She became a life-spring to those who passed through her home or sat under her ministry. I was challenged by the account of Polly Wigglesworth (ch.11) encouraging her husband in his pursuit of God, and of Mary Boddy who was used by God so significantly to release the river of Pentecost through Smith Wigglesworth. I was warmed also to read of the Spirit filled secretaries (ch.8) who testified publicly to their own Baptism in the Spirit and lived it out in daily administrative service at the heart of the Revival. In dealing with masses of correspondence and producing *Confidence* magazine, their infectious faith and joy at God's ways and working, impacted thousands of lives.

At this point I feel like the writer of Hebrews – "What more shall I say? I do not have time to tell of ..." all the others! Read about them here for yourself and pray we may see many more such women raised up in our day!

Faith Forster
December 2006

Dedication

This Book Is Dedicated
to

the women of River Church in The Thames Valley, United Kingdom
who, a hundred years downstream, are seeking to demonstrate the
truths exemplified by these forgotten women
and to
the women of Wellspring Christian Fellowship, Bweyogerere,
Kampala, Uganda

My thanks
to
Chris Forster, leader of River Church who made this book possible
and to the editorial team for their insights and suggestions
and to
Tina Daniels whose genealogical research proved invaluable in
bringing hidden things to light and helped fill in some of the gaps

Introduction

This book is for all believers, men and women, across the denominations and those in none. If you can testify to a dynamic, life changing experience with the Holy Spirit (and even if you can't) this book is for you. It is not just for those who name themselves Pentecostals.

The distinctive message of Pentecostal tradition is the blessing of the Baptism in the Holy Spirit as a definite experience subsequent to conversion accompanied by the sign of tongues (*glossolalia*). It is a gift for every believer. Today, this term has become nuanced among Spirit filled believers. If your experience varies from this classic rendition please don't put the book down but keep reading. These women are part of your history too.

After nearly two thousand years the stream that flowed down through the generations from the upper room gained momentum in the early years of the 20th century birthing a move of the Spirit which erupted on the world wide scene like a great river. Today there are around six hundred million Pentecostal / Charismatic / Spirit filled believers.

In Britain the revival began in the Church of England in September 1907. Many of the stories you will read took place in a northern, working class parish and that is a fact that needs restating and may surprise many.

This book has been latent in my spirit for over six years. I have endeavoured to give factual information about these ladies' lives and draw out a relevance and significance that still speaks today. It was born when I was studying for a master's degree which involved researching the contribution of women's ministry in the early years of Pentecostalism in Britain. I discovered that there was a paucity of material about them and I had to glean nearly all my information from primary sources. I wanted to use my studies in a way that would benefit the church as a whole and move us on and this is the result.

In order to make the contents flow and be easily accessible I have kept end notes to a minimum. However all the contents can be substantiated and I list my sources at the end of the book.

The first and last chapters act as the bread in the sandwich holding the corporate lives of these women together. I wrote much of their contents during a three year period I was living in Uganda. On returning to the UK in 2004 I found that many of the ideas I have expressed were hot topics among Christians here and I believe they are things the Holy Spirit wants to emphasise at this time.

My prayer is that this book will provide a link for Spirit filled believers today with those Spirit filled believers of the past. Writing about their lives is not just a good idea or nostalgic trip because 2007 is the centennial of the Pentecostal Movement in Britain. Anniversaries are generally times to remember and reflect on God's dealings in our lives so let past and present flames come together and create a fire.

Diana Chapman
January 2007

1

Bringing Hidden Things to Light

*'They tunnel through the rock; their eyes see all
its treasures. They search the sources of the rivers
and bring hidden things to light.'*

Job 28:10-11

The Pentecostal waters flowed powerfully around the globe at the beginning of the last century erupting almost simultaneously in different countries. It has been said that this world wide revival 'was rocked in the cradle of little Wales', 'bought up in India' and became 'full grown in Los Angeles'[1]. If that is the case it also had family all over the British Isles.

In this country, the 'charismatic moment' of the revival movement was between 1907 and 1914 and as in all revivals, women, unfettered by institutionalism, seized the day. They were strong, knew their God and empowered by the Holy Spirit, did exploits *(Daniel 11:32 KJV).*

We read of women who pioneered in ministry, lead churches and were popular speakers at conventions. They were often the first to receive the Baptism of the Holy Spirit.

This book is a journey back to the source of the river to bring those hidden things to light. Our eyes will see all the treasures. We will read of stories of women who have largely been forgotten and yet whose lives speak today.

Following the Pentecostal revival at Azusa Street, Los Angeles in April 1906 another well opened on these shores a year later. The hub of the outpouring in 1907 was in the parish of All Saints', Sunderland where the Revd. Alexander Alfred Boddy and his wife Mary together hosted this move of God.

The annual Sunderland Conventions fanned the flames of revival and the magazine *Confidence*[2] spread the Pentecostal message world wide. Its pages are full of examples of women whose lives were impacted by the Baptism of the Holy Spirit, enabling them to speak in tongues and fall deeper in love with their Lord and Saviour Jesus Christ.

One can only be moved by their passion and determination to spread the Gospel message, believing as they did that they were living in the time of the latter rain and the near return of the Lord.

The Roll Call

We will remember wife and mother Catherine Price who challenges us in our pursuit of God and Mary Boddy, Mother of British Pentecostalism, greatly used of God yet cautions to keep our focus on Jesus; Margaret Cantel who opened not just her heart but her home to the Lord and Lydia Walshaw who knew that true Christianity has to be worked out in the workshops and busy places of life; American Carrie Judd Montgomery, a woman of faith who pioneered healing homes and Scottish church planter Christine Beruldsen; the eminently capable Eleanor Crisp who poured out her life into a generation of missionaries and the fiery Polly Wigglesworth, a preacher in her own right and wife of the legendary Smith. Unknown and unheralded women of the revival are represented by 'The Secretaries' at Sunderland, Margaret Scott and Mabel Howell who just worked hard and those intrepid Missionary Ladies who paid such a price as they took the Gospel to the ends of the earth.

Pushing Boundaries

This spiritual awakening was against the backdrop of Edwardian Britain. King Edward VII ruled from 1901 to 1910 and the era is sometimes extended to include the years to the end of the First World War in 1918. They were days of empire, cultural expansion and missionary endeavour. Rapid industrialization coupled with enlightenment thinking were creating an environment for social, economic and political change. Women were pushing traditional social boundaries seen most clearly in the suffrage movement.

The majority of our women would count themselves among the burgeoning middle classes and this gave them the means to travel and take full advantage of the new opportunities afforded them.

It's Happening Again!

Two thousand years after the hundred and twenty in the upper room were filled with the Holy Spirit and began to speak in other tongues it was happening all over again. What excitement! Tongues was a gift that had been largely lost to the church but now men and women who were caught up in this move of the Spirit saw themselves back on God's prophetic calendar. They believed they were living in the last days and that the Holy Spirit had been given in power to enable them to take the Gospel to the ends of the earth before the coming of the Lord.

The former rain had been poured out on the day of Pentecost and now two thousand years later they were living at the time of the latter rain sent by God to bring in the harvest *(Deuteronomy 11:14, Joel 2:23)*.

The significance of Peter's words again rang true two millennia after he had addressed the crowd in Jerusalem, *'This is what was spoken of by the prophet Joel...'*

> *'In the last days, God says, I will pour out My Spirit upon all people. Your sons and daughters will prophesy, your young men will see visions and your old men will dream dreams. Even on My servants both men and women, I will pour out My Spirit in those days, and they will prophesy. I will show wonders in heaven above and signs on earth below, blood and*

*fire and billows of smoke. The sun will be turned to darkness
and the moon to blood before the coming of the great and
glorious day of the Lord. And everyone who calls on the name
of the Lord will be saved' (Joel 2:28-29, Acts 2:17-21).*

The 'Charismatic Moment'

This is a term given to the initial stages of a religious movement before
institutional forces replace charisma as the driving force. Just as the
above verses heralded the 'charismatic moment' for the early church
so they ushered in a unique time for the 20th century believers. The
Holy Spirit had been given equally to men and women on the day of
Pentecost and in the pages of the New Testament we read of anointed
women functioning alongside their brothers in Christ. The Apostle Paul
called them his fellow workers. There were women leaders, prophets,
evangelists, pastors, teachers and yes, apostles. (Paul actually affirmed
women in leadership and gifting). So it's not surprising that as women
in the last century were baptised in the Holy Spirit their anointing
made room for them in a variety of similar ways.

Keeping The Light Burning

Since New Testament days there had always been a remnant keeping
the flames of revival alive. Down through history women have played
a prominent part in revival movements. Following the Montanist
revival in the 2nd and 3rd centuries noted for its prophetesses, the
abbeys of Europe kept the light burning through the Dark Ages. The
Protestant Reformation (1517) bought a measure of leveling with its
emphasis on the Priesthood of Believers.

Then a series of revivals began to elevate women allowing their
voice to be heard. Parallels have been drawn between the Anabaptists
of the 16th century and modern Pentecostalism. They, too, stressed
the Prophethood of Believers where the Holy Spirit had freedom to
minister through men and women alike. In the 17th century Quakers
were the fastest growing movement in the western world and their
defining theological principle of the inner light propelled women
preachers across Britain and other nations especially to the New
World. Methodist women of the 18th century found an ally in John

Wesley who, when asked why he encouraged women preachers said, 'Because God owns them in the conversion of sinners and who am I that I should withstand God'[3]. Women were prominent in the Trans-Atlantic evangelical revivals of the 19th century and their voices rang loud and clear in a plethora of reform societies.

By the time Holiness teaching took hold in this country finding expression in the Keswick Movement and Salvation Army, a tradition of women preachers and teachers was well established providing a platform for our Pentecostal sisters.

Just prior to the 1907 outpouring in Britain women had been largely responsible for spreading the fires in the valleys of Wales in 1904. The following year, in India, a converted Brahmin woman, Pandita Ramabai, was used by God to facilitate an amazing outpouring of the Holy Spirit which started among girls in her orphanage. A lady, Agnes Ozman, was a forerunner of the 1906 revival in America. She spoke in tongues in 1901 some five years before the flood gates opened in Los Angeles. At Azusa Street women ministered with the men and went out across the country carrying the Pentecostal blessing with them.

Getting The Job Done

It is a well documented fact of revivals that 'getting the job done' becomes more important than who is doing it. Revivals are times of great urgency. This allows for women, often young women and even children to respond freely to the stirrings of the Spirit without restrictions and with great success.

At these times the prophetic nature of ministry takes ascendance over the more priestly elements. Authority is grounded in experience rather than in religious doctrine and tradition. Anointing and gifting become the important criteria for leadership and ministry rather than gender.

As revivals are 'managed' or become second generation or as the original leaders die (as John Wesley of the Methodist Revival) or step down for what ever reason (as Evan Roberts of the Welsh Revival) or national events loom large and overtake (as is the case of the First World War and the Pentecostal Revival), the initial stages of the revival cease and this is where there is the danger of institutionalism with its negative effect on the ministry of women.

Bad News - Good News

The question then arises, 'How can we perpetuate what God is (or worse, *was*) doing?' The answer to this question often marks the beginning of a denomination with its inherent structures and positions. Often bad news for women.

This is why in the 'charismatic moment' of a revival, the question needs to be addressed, 'How can we facilitate what God is doing?' The wind blows wherever it pleases but it can be harnessed for increased effect.

It is inevitable that structures will be put in place even in times of revival. The creation of the world shows a God of order. But built into that order is the notion of quantum change, a randomness that we see even in the natural world. We cannot box God into our thinking. If we do, we will remain in the box while the Holy Spirit is moving outside! The only institutional form that we can consider are flexible wineskins to hold the new wine coupled with an attitude of humility. This is good news for women.

One In Christ

The heady days of revival are characterized by the breaking down of barriers whether they be ethnic, social, gender or even ecclesiastical in accordance with the words of the Apostle Paul, *'There is neither Jew nor Gentile, neither slave nor free, neither male nor female, for you are all one in Christ Jesus' (Gal. 3:28).*

In racial conscious American society it was noted at Azusa that 'the colour line was washed away by the blood'[4]. At gatherings of Pentecostals in Sunderland there was evident harmony and equality between nationalities, denominations, social class and men and women even in the class conscious Edwardian society.

A Precarious Pathway

As the early Pentecostal leaders in the fledgling movement walked the precarious pathway between control and anarchy the ministry of women continued to flourish. From time to time statements would be issued on doctrinal points or there would be warnings against false teachers printed in the magazine *Confidence*. Overseers and boards, titles and positions had no place in the early days as the Holy Spirit raised up whom He willed. Authority was validated by the anointing of God on a person's life regardless of gender.

These early leaders, both men and women carried the anointing with them as they travelled between different centres strengthening the work and engaging in evangelism. It was noted at the time, 'The Holy Spirit is clearly leading on very simple lines these days, more in harmony with primitive Christianity'.

The Demise

All the more surprising then that in June 1914 a topic on the agenda at the Sunderland Convention was *A Woman's Place in the Church*. Instead of there being a celebration of their invaluable contribution this was a discussion which focused on limiting their ministry. Although Alexander Boddy seemed to be happy with the status quo, ministerial colleague Pastor Jonathan Paul from Berlin was determined to place what he considered scriptural restrictions on women especially in the roles of teaching and leadership. For several years there had been a Pentecostal Advisory Board meeting annually at the Sunderland Conventions and now it was becoming more authoritative.

Although well meaning and sincere, it is tragic that more credence was not given to the work of the Spirit in these ladies recognizing that it was God himself who had raised them up and was using them to great effect. Father, Son and Spirit speak with one voice. It's impossible for the Lord to empower a woman and then restrict her with His own Word. In effect this is what they were doing. No policy statement was issued but doubts had been voiced and underlying attitudes began to surface.

This was just before the outbreak of the First World War in 1914 and for women in the Pentecostal Movement in Britain, things were never to be the same again. The 'charismatic moment' was over and with it the demise of their ministries. History once again was repeating itself.

Shine, Women, Shine!

Many women had been already been involved teaching and preaching in Holiness circles. They didn't just appear on the scene in 1907. The term 'The Baptism in the Holy Spirit' was initially used by John Wesley's theologian, John Fletcher, to explain a second blessing of 'being made holy' or sanctification. An American Holiness teacher, Phoebe Palmer whilst on a four year speaking tour of Britain from 1859-1863 began to teach that the experience of the Baptism in the Holy Spirit gave power for service. In the Welsh Revival a greater emphasis was on the power to testify. The verses from *Acts 2:17-18* gave these women permission to prophesy whether it be in testimony, teaching, preaching or speaking out a word that the Holy Spirit had given them.

It was not until the gift of speaking in tongues was restored in greater measure to the church and seen as the sign of Baptism in the Holy Spirit that theological minds began to claim this heralded a restoration of the days of the Acts of the Apostles. The very seriousness with which early Pentecostals read the New Testament, taking everything literally, resulted in ambiguities for women. Whilst acknowledging that scripture gave permission for daughters to prophesy, it also told women to keep silent in the church. The above meeting was an attempt to reconcile verses which on face value do seem contradictory and in many cases appear to narrow a woman's sphere of ministry.

It is not the function of this book to exegete the so called 'difficult passages' but to highlight the importance of having a biblical theology where there is a harmony between the Spirit and Word. As Harvey Cox observes in his book *Fire From Heaven*,[5] 'Wherever the original Pentecostal fire breaks through the flame extinguishing literalist theology, women shine'. Women did indeed shine in those early days of the 20th century Pentecostal revival.

Before some of you may be tempted at this point to throw this book against the wall I am not advocating some new feminist hermeneutic. My friend, Chris Forster puts it this way, 'Once we lose the inspiration of the Spirit we start approaching Scripture looking for laws rather than life'.

Bottled At Source

In front of me as I write is a bottle of water. On the label is written, 'Pure spring water, bottled at source'. This water was 'captured' before it became polluted further down stream. 'Estuary water' would hardly be a best seller on the supermarket shelves!

The nearer to the source of a river you go, the purer the water. So it is with the moves of God in the earth. The nearer to the source or beginnings of a movement the purer the intention of the Spirit is seen before man manages, controls or even digs his own channel.

The beginning of the Pentecostal Movement in Britain was initiated by a powerful move of God. It was a time of divine intervention in the affairs of man. It was the source of a river of blessing that has continued to flow. If we are to gain greater insight into the heart and mind of God we need to pay attention to what was happening at the source. The Holy Spirit gave permission for women to function according to their anointing and gifting and function they did! We need to take care to loose those things on earth that are loosed in heaven or we may find ourselves fighting against God.

Sapphires And Nuggets Of Gold

With all this in mind these verses from Job give a prophetic context to this book.

> *'There is a mine for silver and a place where gold is refined. Iron is taken from the earth, and copper is smelted from ore. Miners put an end to the darkness; they search out the farthest recesses for ore in the blackest darkness. Far from human dwellings they cut a shaft, in places untouched by human feet far from other people they dangle and sway. The earth, from which food comes, is transformed below as by fire;* **sapphires come from its rocks, and its dust contains nuggets of gold.** *No bird of prey knows that hidden path, no falcon's eye has seen it. Proud beasts do not set foot on it, and no lion prowls there. The miner's hands assault the flinty rock and lay bare the roots of the mountains. They tunnel through the rock; their eyes see all its treasures.* **They search the sources of the rivers and bring hidden things to light'.**

Job 28:1-11

What Is God saying?

1.   There is a mine, there is a place to dig *(v. 1)*
2.   These are forgotten places *(v. 4)*
3.   Work is involved
        Tunnel through the rock *(v. 10)*
        Search the farthest recesses *(v. 3)*
        Assault the flinty rock *(v. 9)*
        Lay bare the roots of the mountains *(v. 9)* 'roots'
        being a poetic expression emphasizing great depth
4.   Sapphires come from its rocks and its dust contains
        nuggets of gold *(v. 6)*
5.   The eyes of the person who tunnels through the rock will
        see all the treasures *(v. 10)*

I've done the digging and my eyes have seen the sapphires and nuggets of gold. Hidden things have come to light and it is these I will share with you in the following pages.

Bones And Stones

Leonard Sweet in his book *Soul Tsunami*,[6] a commentary on post modernity, talks about carrying the 'bones and stones' of memory with us, 'the memory of our past and the memory of our ancestors' He says that 'to abandon the past is to forget what we know'. Understanding our roots can help us find direction, inspiration and fresh food for the journey.

As well as being rooted and grounded in God we can draw sustenance from knowing our spiritual ancestry. We are not orphans but have Spirit filled mothers (as well as fathers) of faith ready to teach us by example. Women who were confident in their beliefs, had faith in their God, were not afraid to take the road less travelled and who encourage us to do the same.

God thinks remembering, or rather not forgetting, is important. Moses took the past with him into the future when he took Joseph's bones out of Egypt. The Israelites left piles of stones in the Promised

Land so a future generation when asking the question, 'What do these stones mean?' could be told the stories of deliverance. Jesus said that the story of Mary, whose devotion touched his heart, would be told wherever the Gospel was preached in memory of her *(Mark 14:9)*.

The Psalmist says, *'... I will utter hidden things, things from of old – what we have heard and known, what our fathers have told us. We will not hide them from our children; we will tell the next generation...' (Psalm 78:2-4, NIV)*.

What better time to remember these forgotten women. As I write it's the year of the centennial of the 20th century Pentecostal revival. We remember not for nostalgic reasons but to commend His works, speak of His power, tell of His deliverance, pass on revelation, encourage faith and to declare that we as Spirit filled believers stand in a line of blessing that belongs to us. But before it can belong to us we have to know about it.

We are not meant to live our lives in a 21st century vacuum, people and stories from the past are important and help shape our future.

Standing In Line

These godly women at the source of the Pentecostal river are our heritage. We stand in their generational line. We are further downstream but the flow is from the same source.

The closing verses of the Old Testament book of Malachi speak of a turning of the hearts of the parents to their children, and the hearts of the children to their parents *(Malachi 4:5-6)*. I believe that as well as referring to natural parents an application can be made to include wider generational continuity. As we turn our hearts to learn and listen we will see more than just quaint cameos from the past.

There were many women whose names and deeds have long been forgotten by man but have not been forgotten by God. They are written in His scroll of remembrance. They are His jewels *(Malachi 3:16-17, NIV)*. They are the many 'nursing mothers' who kept the testimony alive in its infant years. The ones whose stories I have chosen to tell have a core theme running through their lives which is as relevant today as it was then.

Cameos Of Forgotten Women

Catherine Price has gone down in history as the first person to speak in tongues in the 20th century Pentecostal outpouring in Britain. She was a woman of prayer who, like Mary, cautions us to follow Jesus, not the blessing. Her life was given to pursuing intimacy with Christ.

Mary Boddy was a key player and deserves the title 'The Mother of British Pentecostalism'. Not only a wife and mother she was a teacher, preacher and writer. In July 1908, *Confidence* reports, 'The Vicarage was a busy place with people coming and going…with sick bodies and tired souls and all are helped'. She ministered healing and prayed for many to receive the Baptism of the Holy Spirit including Smith Wigglesworth. She left a legacy but more than that her life was 'Taken up with Jesus' and her writings challenge us to rekindle our passion to glorify Jesus over and above our spiritual experiences.

Many women opened their homes as 'Homes of Rest' and for meetings. One such woman was Margaret Cantel. It was said that being in her meetings one could imagine they were in similar first century meetings in Ephesus or Corinth, especially when spiritual gifts were manifested.

More down to earth was Lydia Walshaw who after experiencing the Baptism of the Holy Spirit said that the love of God enabled her to love the unlovely and 'throw her arms around them in all their dirt and sin'. She was a sought after speaker and a leader.

American, Carrie Judd Montgomery was a woman of faith and an influential visitor to our shores. Editor of *Triumphs of Faith* for sixty six years she ministered Divine Healing and pioneered healing homes where the sick could receive prayer.

A strong woman, Christina Berulsden was a church planter. She led a Pentecostal mission in the city of Edinburgh and at Leith docks, Scotland. It was written of her, 'Her family showed to the world whose they are and whom they serve'.

Revivals need 'behind the scenes' workers and 'The Secretaries' at Sunderland, Miss Margaret Scott and Miss Mabel Howell, worked hard providing an indispensable service distributing the magazine *Confidence* until the Lord gave them a ministry of their own amongst the poor.

Formidable Eleanor Crisp was the principle of the Pentecostal Missionary Union Women's Testing and Training Home and was formative in training a generation of missionaries. A notable speaker, she also had an impressive gift of interpretation of tongues.

Many women paid a high price in missionary service facing disease and death on foreign fields as they took the Gospel to the ends of the earth. They were dubbed, 'Missionaries of the one way ticket'[7] because of their belief in an imminent rapture, but it could also be said it was because some never came home.

Polly Wigglesworth was the wife of Smith, whose world wide ministry of signs and wonders is legendary. A lesser known fact is that for most of their married life, Polly was the more prominent of the two, a fiery preacher who 'put down the net' while Smith would be at the altar 'landing the fish'.

As we have noted all this was taking place in Edwardian Britain. In this period, ladies, especially British ones, were more often than not referred to only by their title, Mrs. or Miss. Today we find this rather formal so I have taken the liberty of referring to them by their first name, unheard of in that era. In some cases detective work in the 1901 census was needed to even find out what they were. But I feel that this makes their lives more accessible and their personalities somehow more human.

Living Letters

These are women who by their example and writings are living letters. They were role models to a generation. No one would want to return to this past era but in their own unique ways they had captured something of the heartbeat of God and gave expression to that in their lives and ministries.

Now, at the beginning of the 21st century, God's heartbeat for the world has not changed. Let's brush the dust off their lives and allow these bold, godly women to be our inspiration as we are, today, one hundred years closer to the coming of our Lord.

---

1   Frank Bartleman, *Azusa Street,* (Gainsville: Bridge-Logos, 1980), 22

2   *Confidence* was published from 1908 to 1926. It was edited by Alexander Boddy and sent out from Sunderland until 1922.

3   Chilcote Paul, *John Wesley and the Women Preachers of Early Methodism,* (London: Scarecrow Press, 1991), 182

4   Frank Bartleman, *Azusa Street,* (Gainsville: Bridge-Logos, 1980), xxvii

5   Harvey Cox, *Fire from Heaven,* (London: Cassell, 1996), 125

6   Leonard Sweet, *Soul Tsunami,* (Grand Rapids: Zondervan, 1999), 88-91

7   Vinson Synan, *The Century of the Holy Spirit,* (Nashville: Thomas Nelson Publishers, 2001), 6

2

Catherine Price
Pursuing The Presence Of God

'Dwell deep…these are days in which we
need to be hidden in Christ'

Catherine Price

Catherine Sophia Price has gone down in Pentecostal history as the first person to be baptised in the Holy Spirit with the accompanying sign of tongues in connection with the 20th century outpouring in the British Isles. She was a woman of prayer who sought intimacy with God over and above manifestations of the Spirit.

Behold The Lamb

At the beginning of the year 1909, two years after her personal Pentecost, Catherine asked the Lord to give her a message that would help not just herself but others in all circumstances of life, whether they be difficulties, trials or joys. As she waited quietly, a still small voice said, 'Behold the Lamb'. She recalls that in quietness before Him each word was quickened until it thrilled her whole being. This extract is taken from that message as it appeared in *Confidence* October 1909.

'What unutterable depths of love, tenderness and compassion one sees as they gaze upon that blessed face! Has not your poor heart often cried, 'Oh that I were more like Him?' Then, dear one, obey His Word and 'Behold the Lamb!' It is a command. You may not see Him in an actual vision, but Jesus will be revealed to you as you obey, and beholding you will be changed *(2 Corinthians 3:17)*. In these days there is such a tendency, even amongst God's dear children, to behold everything and everybody save the Lamb – meetings, people, an experience, a joy, a blessing, that will never truly satisfy them nor the Lord Jesus.

The very simplicity of the command stumbles us. He will reveal Himself to you in a way you have never dreamt of if you make this your constant occupation. Nothing must be held back if you would see His face and be conformed to His glorious image. First taking Him by faith in the fullness of the Holy Ghost to dwell within the secret hidden chambers of your soul; then, whether you walk, or stand, or eat, or drink, or sleep or wake, He will be revealed in you…Beloved, worship, adore, live in His presence every moment'.

It was based on the scripture in *John 1:35-39* which she believed to be 'a sweet picture of the soul desiring to know God intimately'. She gave this talk to the prayer group that used to meet at her house and recalls that afterwards the Holy Spirit was poured out on all who were present as He had done so many times before.

First To Receive Tongues

Catherine was a woman who knew God and was deeply in love with Jesus. She was one of God's chosen vessels who like Mary, the mother of our Lord, was highly favoured. As we have noted, her life displayed the sign of the first fruits of the Pentecostal Revival, speaking in tongues. Rather like Agnes Ozman, the American lady who spoke in tongues some five years before the Azusa outpouring, Catherine was a forerunner of Pentecost in Britain eight months before the well opened at Sunderland. We all have heard it said that God has no favourites and that is true yet we know that His heart is touched in response to a life that hungers and thirsts after His presence.

In writing about Catherine's experience Alexander Boddy, vicar of All Saints' leaves us with the impression that she was the first woman to speak in tongues in Britain's history but that is not the case. There was tongues speaking associated with the Irvingites in the mid 19th century both in London and Scotland and occasionally in American Holiness preacher, Phoebe Palmer's meetings on her four year speaking tour of these Isles in the 1860s. And it's difficult not to believe it happened on numerous other undocumented occasions.

The News Travelled

Following the Welsh Revival of 1904-5, prayer groups had sprung up all over the British Isles where earnest and constant prayer rose to heaven for revival. News of the happenings at the Azusa Street Mission, where people travelled to from all over the world to receive their Baptism with signs following, heightened expectation and the cry went out on these shores, 'Send another Pentecost'. From 1906 the *Apostolic Faith* magazine carried news from Azusa documenting the events in Los Angeles as they unfolded and was devoured by hungry British Christians.

Her Prayer Group Begins

Catherine started one such prayer group in her home some six months before she received her Pentecost. It would seem from letters to *Apostolic Faith* that there were three people that gathered together to cry out to God, a man, J. Himners and a lady called Mary Martin and Catherine. However it was not at one of the meetings that she received the Baptism in the Holy Spirit but when she was alone in prayer late one night as was her custom.

She said that the experience happened 'after months of inexpressible yearnings and waiting upon God.' She had been attending some special meetings and on this particular night she relates that the words that had been spoken by the preacher kept ringing in her ear, *'Faithful is He that calleth you who also will do it' (1 Thess 5:24 KJV).* Filled with joy mingled with faith she sought the Lord.

Her Night With The King

This particular night was early in the New Year 1907. It was past midnight and the rest of the household had retired. In order to do justice to the wonderful experience she had with the Lord the testimony can only be told in her own words.

> 'Praise and adoration filled my soul…the joy was flowing… That night I seemed to lie down in His almighty arms like a weary little child. The last cord that bound me to earth was broken, and that was a little anxiety concerning my home and dear ones. I gave them up to Him and just rested absolutely in Him.
>
> While praising Him I had a vision of Jesus upon the cross. It was dark. He extended His arms to me and said, 'Come to me.' Oh the unutterable love and compassion in His voice. I obeyed and groaned in the Spirit, seeming to suffer with Him. Then the darkness fled and I was raised with Him in glory. Involuntarily I threw up my arms to praise Him and suddenly they seemed charged with electricity and a power came on me and I praised Him in another tongue.
>
> He immediately gave the interpretation, which was, 'Glory to Jesus – the bleeding Lamb'. The next morning the Holy Ghost came in much power, causing me to laugh as I had never done in my life being very matter-of-fact and unemotional and speaking in four or five languages, sometimes giving the interpretation. For one and a half hours this continued. I was quite powerless. The glory of God filled my soul, sometimes the deepest anguish of heart at the cross. What I felt and realised of the sorrow and love of Jesus was beyond expression, finding vent only in another tongue. Glory to His Name!'

Glory to His Name indeed! What an inspiring description of her 'night with the King' and like Esther, things were never the same again. She walked daily with the King of kings and learned to pursue Him, cherishing those intimate moments in His presence.

Her Home And Her Dear Ones

She describes the sound of the tongues she spoke out that night as 'soft, flowing and beautiful' but they weren't silent. In reading her testimony one wonders whether the rest of her family slept through this occasion oblivious to the fact that this dear lady was making history. I can only assume that when she refers to her anxiety about her 'home and dear ones' that maybe they didn't totally share her religious views or it could be that her children were sickly.

Like so many of our forgotten women, little is known about their family lives. Catherine was born in Newington, London in 1877 so at the time she received her Baptism she was thirty years old. Her husband Llewellyn was thirty five and although he was born in London was obviously of Welsh extraction. It was an upwardly mobile family since in 1901 his occupation was a printer's foreman yet not many years later he was a bank manager. She had her three children in quick succession, her first child, Wilfred, being born in 1900. It is my conjecture that Llewellyn came from a background of nonconformity in the chapels of Wales. He served as secretary to the Brixton YMCA and printed religious pamphlets for Pentecostal leaders Alexander Boddy and Cecil Polhill. This information suggests he was a Christian yet he is never mentioned in any of her writings as having a part in these meetings. Catherine lived until 1956 when she died at the age of seventy nine on 15th September at her daughter's home in Carshalton, Surrey.

One pictures her as a respectable wife and mother who longs for her family to love the Lord in the way she does. In middle class Edwardian society of the time it was not unusual for the woman of the home to be involved in 'religious activities' and to devote herself to good works in accordance with what was believed to be the 'natural piety' of the female sex, while the husband occupied himself in the man's sphere of business and politics.

The Spirit Falls Again

So after this extraordinary night, the next evening found Catherine once more at the special meetings where the Spirit came on her again causing her to speak in three or four languages with the interpretation. As she sat there the Lord gave her a vision of the Lamb of God enthroned but pleading with His people to humble themselves. She felt she should tell this to the congregation but when she did she could only speak in tongues. A minister sitting near her asked her if she knew the language and if she didn't would she ask the Lord for the interpretation. She spoke out the burden of her heart in English and great conviction followed and some were anointed with the Holy Spirit. One lady was healed from a stammer as she responded to the word of the Lord given through Catherine.

The meetings continued the next night and the Holy Spirit continued to fall, anointing many as they sat in their seats.

Prayer Meetings Continue

Catherine continued the prayer meetings at her house at 14 Akerman Road, Brixton in South East London which were considered by Pentecostal leader and historian Donald Gee to be the first 'definitely Pentecostal' meetings in Britain. She wrote, 'A few of us who met for prayer at the beginning will never forget the awe of God's holy presence in the room when everything gently rocked. They had been reading the scripture in Acts where it says, *'After they prayed, the place where they were meeting was shaken' (Acts 4:31)*. This occurred on two occasions and the people present as well as the room shook. The second time it happened she felt she had grieved the Lord because she opened her eyes to look around. The comment she makes is interesting believing 'the Lord…does not want us to be occupied with manifestations of His presence but with Himself alone'.

Writing of the summer of 1907, Alexander said that he knew of half a dozen or so in Britain who were baptised in the Holy Spirit and spoke in tongues and included in that number those who had been blessed 'in the house of that child of God, Mrs. Price'. He called them, 'The little band in Brixton'.

J. Hinmers, one of the original prayer group was with Catherine the day after she received the Baptism in the Holy Spirit. He wrote to *Apostolic Faith* validating her experience saying that he had heard her speak in several tongues and that now all three of them had received 'the evidence'. He wrote about the changes in their lives, how the only book they wanted to read now was the Bible and about the 'solemn yet heavenly times they had speaking and singing in tongues'.

A year later in 1908 we read that the meetings continued to be held in her home. Mary Martin wrote to *Apostolic Faith* in January 1908 about the supernatural times they were having. 'People are coming from far and near, and no one has ever been invited. They just hear how God is working and come…Several have had blessed anointings, outpourings of the Spirit and revelations of Jesus Christ'.

A Home Of Rest

Where was her husband while all this was going on? Llewellyn would probably not have minded the prayer gatherings in the home as long as he had an orderly, respectable household but as well as holding prayer meetings it was open to visitors. Like others dotted around the country this 'Home of Rest' provided hospitality for Pentecostal ministers and those attending conventions as well as missionaries passing through the country. We know that one particular American missionary, A.H. Post stayed at the Price residence for quite a while since he gave his address c/o Mrs. Price at Akerman Road. Respected Pentecostal leaders such as Smith Wigglesworth were also known to have taken advantage of Catherine's home from home.

By January 1912 the Price family had moved to Oak Lodge, 1 Horsford Road, Brixton where as well as Pentecostal meetings being held each week, this house too was a 'Home of Rest'. The meetings and the home were advertised in *Confidence*.

With Pentecostal meetings taking place weekly for the last five years in the home and men and women of God staying there, it's hard to believe that her husband wasn't involved in some way. But it's clear that whatever his standing before the Lord it was Catherine that led this work of God in her home.

A Respected Leader

Alexander Boddy called her, an 'honoured servant of God' and she was counted among the inner circle of leaders. When at a camp meeting in Ohio in 1909, he spoke to the gathered crowd specifically about the work of God in Sunderland, Brixton and London. She attended significant occasions like the opening of the Pentecostal Missionary Union's Ladies' Training Home and various conferences. In November 1908, The London Declaration was written setting out the beliefs of the emerging Pentecostal Movement in regard to the Baptism in the Holy Spirit. It stated, 'What we teach concerning the evidence and the results'. Catherine Price's signature appeared at the bottom among thirty other respected Pentecostal leaders of the day.

The declaration continued 'there was no hint in Holy Scripture that signs and miracles were to cease or that gifts were to be withdrawn from the Body of Christ'. Whilst assenting to all the tenets of the statement she would have particularly endorsed the concluding sentence. 'It should be clearly understood that the Baptism in the Holy Ghost is the 'gate into', and not the 'goal' of a true and full Christian life'.

Access To His Presence

Catherine kept in touch with Alexander Boddy and the work of God that was going on in the parish of All Saints', Sunderland. She heard all about the first Sunderland Conventions from friends of hers that had attended. In a letter to Alexander she asked that if they had learnt anything fresh that would be of help to her little group to pass it on.

It would appear that she was concerned that manifestations were taking the place of simply enjoying the presence of God. She wrote, 'Some dear ones are straining every nerve to receive tongues and letting their minds dwell on very little else, and they get tongues. But oh, the divine fellowship with the Father and His Son Jesus Christ seem to be lacking. The thoughts are drawn to the individual instead of inducing adoration to Jesus'. For Catherine, tongues were not an end in themselves but a means of fellowshipping with Jesus and a way to access His presence.

Dwell Deep

She also expressed concern that some were relying on the messages given in tongues with interpretation rather than the Word of God to direct their lives. In days when God was speaking directly through His Spirit, the Word was sometimes not thought to be so necessary.

It's interesting, too, that the first woman to speak in tongues in Britain in the 20th century said that 'we must not allow it to be said that no one has received the Spirit except those who have spoken in tongues'. She said that the fellowship she has had with some of the Lord's Spirit filled children would contradict this statement.

As in all revivals there was a mixture of the real and the counterfeit. She recognised this cautioning the need for reality. Catherine's advice was to 'dwell deep'. These were days, she said, when they needed to be hidden in Christ.

Hidden In Christ

What we can glean regarding Catherine's life challenges us. She is a lady whose own life was truly 'hidden in Christ' and her secret, 'to dwell deep'. *Psalm 42:7* says, *'Deep calls to deep'*. The only way to enjoy any meaningful relationship is to spend time with the other person so that the veneer of superficiality is penetrated. It's only then true intimacy can begin. There is no easy way to get to know God, time is required.

Psalm 103:7 says, *'He made known His ways to Moses and His deeds known to the people of Israel'*. Moses is called a friend of God. He knew the ways of God. He had spent forty days on the mountain as it was enveloped in the cloud when God gave him the Ten Commandments. In the 'Tent of Meeting' the Lord would speak with Moses face to face as a man would speak to his friend. Intimate moments indeed. The people of Israel could only stand in awe and worship at a distance as they saw the pillar of cloud descend across the entrance when Moses entered the tent. But it was only Moses who had the privilege of the Presence.

This is what he cherished more than all the miracles and manifestations and would not move another step without it. *'If Your Presence does not go with us,'* he said, *'Do not send us up from here' (Exodus 33:15)*. He'd seen all the many miracles of deliverance in Egypt, the parting of the Red Sea, rods turning to snakes. But he knew that if the Presence was with him, God would be there with the miracles when they needed them.

Catherine wrote, 'Beloved, worship, adore, live in His presence every moment'. She had learned the secret of spending time with the Lord. She wrote, 'Jesus hungers to possess us…He thirsts for thirsty souls and has promised to pour floods upon the dry ground and will do so as we learn to stand upon His Word in simple faith'.

Jesus said that He who sees what is done in secret will reward you openly *(Matthew 6:4)* and Catherine's reward for the time she spent in the secret place, the gift of tongues at a time when few if any had received this accompanying sign to the Baptism in the Holy Spirit in the British Isles.

It's still God himself that we must pursue, not the miracles, wonderful as they are. Not the manifestations, exciting as they may be. Not even the gifts that we are told to eagerly desire but the Presence. When our lives are lived in His Presence we have everything.

We don't know too much about Catherine's personal life but the devotion to her Lord shines through her testimonies and letters leaving a mark on the 21st century reader which must challenge our walk with the Lord.

3

Mary Boddy
Taken Up With Jesus

'Get taken up with Jesus…be filled with the Spirit and God will use us. He will bring people to us for blessing and will flow through us to them in rivers of living water'

Mary Boddy

Mary Boddy was the wife of Revd. Alexander Alfred Boddy, vicar of All Saints', Monkwearmouth, Sunderland. As such she was at the hub of the Pentecostal revival in Britain. The couple operated as a ministerial team and together facilitated this move of God that impacted the world. The above quote is taken from a message she gave at the first Sunderland Convention in June 1908 and shows her life's motivation, to glorify Jesus. From this passion flowed her life's work, to bless others and in doing this she left a legacy which impacted future generations.

Testimony Of A Vicar's Wife

We know more about Mary than most of the other early British Pentecostal women because of her unique, high profile position in the movement. Alexander Boddy was proud of his wife and encouraged her to use her gifts and talents to the full. Many of her teachings and addresses were printed at length in *Confidence* and she travelled around the country speaking at various conventions in major cities as well as at the annual Sunderland Convention closer to home.

Through *Confidence*, a series of booklets called *Pentecost at Sunderland* were made available with testimonies of different people who had received the Baptism in the Holy Spirit. Among them was Mary's testimony, *The Testimony of a Vicar's Wife*, which was still being reprinted in 1911.

Because of the blessing she was to seekers who travelled to Sunderland to 'catch the fire', her name is also mentioned in testimonies of many other people including those who later were to become leaders in the movement. She ministered healing and had a special gift of the laying on of hands to help people receive the Baptism in the Holy Spirit.

Foundational Theology

The influence Mary had on early Pentecostal theology has probably been underestimated. Alexander had his hands on the reins in those early days and what he allowed to be taught either in the conventions or in the written pages of *Confidence* became normative. Mary's contribution to both was foundational. Her's was a theology developed through personal experiences of divine healing and Spirit baptism and she delivered her teachings with passion and conviction. It was her healing that had sparked Alexander's interest in the subject.

Fully endorsed and encouraged by her husband she disseminated her views undaunted by opposition. When antagonist Mrs. Jessie Penn-Lewis wrote to Alexander expressing a concern that those who spoke in tongues were victims of demonic deception she especially mentioned his wife. This prompted a sharp response from Mary.

A Godly Young Woman

Mary was born in Scotland in 1858 to a godly family. Her parents, the Revd. and Mrs. Pollock later moved to Yorkshire and she used to accompany her father to the Keswick Conventions. It was here she was exposed to the Holiness teachers of the day with their foundational theology of 'the second blessing' of sanctification. The Pollock household was a place where prayer and love of the Bible nurtured her relationship with God and Mary grew up to enjoy church services and communion. As a clergyman's daughter she had ample opportunity to involve herself in good works to which she gave herself.

Her brother John was a curate at All Saints', Sunderland and it was probably through him she met Alexander, also a regular at Keswick. In 1890 she was invited to sing at one of his many revival services and more went on than just the services because she became his wife in 1891! Mary was in her early thirties and Alexander four years her senior. Within four years she bore three children. May was born in 1892, Jane the following year and James in 1896.

Although working within the Church of England, they were also part of The Pentecostal League, a national organisation based in Sunderland which promoted revival and holiness as the result of the purifying fire of Spirit baptism. Unfortunately, the League later opposed the Spirit's work at All Saints' and pronounced speaking in tongues as demonic.

The Pentecostal League made room for women to teach and preach and at Keswick. Mary would have heard powerful women of God, although they were only allowed to minister in women's meetings. So she had role models to encourage her to embrace her call as well as a husband who had an egalitarian view of ministry.

An Invalid

The early years of her marriage were not easy for Mary and she eventually had a physical breakdown. She developed chronic asthma, bronchitis and 'other weaknesses' which she attributed to her enlarged sphere of church work and increased responsibilities. She also had three youngsters running round the house and a husband who as a member of The Geographical Society enjoyed his trips abroad. Probably the position of the vicarage had more to do with it! Monkwearmouth was on the bleak north east coast of England where sea mists were common and smoke from the region's heavy industry lingered in the air forming an unhelpful cocktail to anyone prone to chest disorders.

Alexander described the church as being 'smoke smitten'. There were busy iron works next to the vicarage and ships being built half a mile away at the mouth of the river Wear. So Mary became, in her own words, 'an invalid' and unable to carry out any of her duties.

A More Excellent Way

Because she hadn't heard of Divine Healing Mary was willing to accept her poor health as God's will in order to discipline her. But, she says, 'God had a more excellent way'. She began to search the Scriptures and after many months of prayer God spoke to her from *John 5:39-40, 'You diligently study the Scriptures that testify about Me because you think that by them you possess eternal life, yet you refuse to come to Me to have life'.*

She records, 'On 23rd February 1899, as I believed the Word and received Jesus to come into me as my physical life, He did so, and I was made whole'. Although she testified many times to her healing and never recanted her beliefs she continued to struggle with ill health. At the Sunderland Convention in 1914 she stood to give her address, the first time she had been able to do so in three years.

Christ Our Life

This experience had a profound effect on her life and from this time on she exercised a healing ministry and taught authoritatively on the subject of Divine Healing. A paradox because she was greatly used by God in the one area that was her weakness. Like the Apostle Paul she learned that when she was weak Christ was her strength *(2 Corinthians 12:9-10).*

Mary's theology was based on the finished work of Christ on the cross. Her central theme was the Christian's union with Christ both in His death and in His life *(Romans 6)*. She explained, because Christ bore our sins and sicknesses and we are 'In Him', sin and sickness should have no part in our lives. Divine health and healing belong to the Christian because Christ is our life.

Throughout the years and in various ways this truth emerges in her teachings. After hearing her teach on this subject at the first Sunderland Convention, one delegate commented, 'Mrs. Boddy has a wonderful gift of explaining our death to sin and our life in Jesus'. At the 1909 Sunderland Convention the delegates wore badges declaring, 'Dead Indeed' and the next year, 'Christ Liveth in Me' no doubt themes influenced by Mary.

It Is Finished

Her theological understanding was rooted in a fresh revelation that the Lord gave her at the time of her healing. She says that God gave her a wonderful vision of Calvary and in *The Testimony of a Vicar's Wife* she writes, 'He showed me the cross, and as I looked on the suffering Saviour, I heard Him say, 'It is finished'. She continues,

> 'The Spirit then caused me to see that at that supreme moment in the world's history, a full, perfect and sufficient sacrifice, oblation and satisfaction for the sins of the *whole* world was made for those who would only believe and receive Him. The Spirit clearly *spoke* saying that this could never be repeated, and could never be upset, but that Satan, from time to time had been and was making people believe it was not true. He also showed me the meaning of *death...*'

By this she means that since we have died 'In Christ' our bodies are simply instruments through which Christ could work. Attitudes such as 'temper, worry and pride' were sins that were part of her old life but now were 'under the blood' and were to be reckoned as such.

Developing Theology

As Mary began to teach on Divine Healing certain nuances developed which are worth mentioning.

When Mary was an invalid she accepted it as discipline from the Lord until the light of God shone on His Word and revealed that Christ was her life and health. She made a perceptive observation, that the discipline of sickness is superseded by the truth of Divine Healing, the more excellent way. In other words Divine Healing does not negate discipline but is a superior truth which God makes available to us experientially.

In 1914 in a talk at the Sunderland Convention she was at pains to make her hearers really understand the revelation of the creative power of the spoken Word of God in relation to healing.

> 'The Word of God will be life in us, and as we speak the Word boldly, He will stretch forth His hands and heal in the name of Jesus only…Let the Word sink into your heart, whether you understand it or not. It is a living thing. The Holy Ghost will quicken it, and it will become life and substance within you. Take the Word of God and don't let the devil take it away. Hold it in your heart. It is a living thing, it is a living thing, it is a living thing – it is life and you will find what you are longing for'.

Pentecost For Britain!

The turn of the 20th century bought with it a heightened expectation for a great move of God. The cry went up from prayer groups around the country, 'Pentecost for Britain'! The spiritual hunger at All Saints' was no exception. Alexander had visited the Welsh Revival in 1904 where Evan Roberts had prophesied, 'The power of the Spirit will sweep over Sunderland'. When Alexander heard of the outpouring of the Spirit in Norway in 1907 he travelled there too, hungry for more of God.

The Boddys and a group of 'seekers after God' waited in prayer for months at the vicarage in Sunderland for the baptism of fire to fall.

They were encouraged at times by signs from heaven. One evening in June 1907 a light filled the room they were in and then lingered over the church roof. Another time, Mary records, a wonderful light fell on her causing her to laugh as she had never done before.

It's ironic that when the fire fell at the beginning of September 1907, Mary was in the south of England. When she returned, Pastor Barratt from Norway had been holding special meetings for ten days and several had been baptised in the Holy Spirit and were speaking in tongues.

Chinese I Think

On the evening after she came home, September 11th, Mary went to the meeting feeling spiritually dry. Pastor Barratt laid hands on her. She recalls the moment in her testimony,

> 'What followed I cannot describe, and it is too sacred to do so, but I knew God had come. Though never unconscious, I was quite oblivious to everyone around, just worshipping, then my mouth began to quiver, my tongue began to move, and a few simple words were uttered, as I yielded to the Holy Ghost. Much to my astonishment, I began to speak in a foreign language – Chinese I think. The Spirit sang through me. The joy and rapture of this pure spiritual worship can never be described. If for no other purpose, I felt at last satisfied that, 'there was no difference between me and them *at the beginning"(Acts 11:15)*.

The meeting lasted until one in the morning and Mary didn't only speak in tongues but sang as well.

Barratt's meetings continued for six weeks and although only twenty five had been filled with the Spirit and spoke in tongues it marked the beginning of the 20th century Pentecostal Revival in Britain. There were two daily meetings, a well was opened, and the thirsty came to drink, especially at the Sunderland Conventions which from 1908 were held annually at Whitsun.

Under Her Hands

Those who have a theology not just born in the Word but in the Spirit's dealings in their lives have a ministry of life. The gift which had been given to Mary as Pastor Barratt laid hands on her, she now imparted to many others as she exercised the ministry of the laying on of hands to receive the Baptism of the Holy Spirit with the sign of speaking in tongues. God used her greatly both in the semi private setting of the vicarage and in conventions around the country. This ministry cannot be underestimated.

The laying on of hands was considered a priestly function in the Church of England but her vicar husband was willing to be experimental and fortunately had a bishop who was an encouraging sympathiser.

Most notable of those who came under her hands shortly after Barratt's visit was Smith Wigglesworth, who was to become known internationally as an 'Apostle of Faith', with a remarkable healing ministry. At that time, he and his wife Polly led a mission in Bradford. In a letter to Mr. and Mrs. Boddy he wrote about the experience saying that he went to Sunderland with a…

> 'holy, breathing cry after this clear manifestation [tongues]…
> At about 11am, Tuesday morning, at All Saints' Vicarage,
> I asked a sister [Mrs. Boddy] to help me to the witness of
> the Baptism of the Holy Ghost. She laid hands on me in the
> presence of a brother. The fire fell and burned in me till the
> Holy Spirit clearly revealed absolute purity before God'.

Apparently the first thing he did after receiving his Baptism was to give Mary Boddy a kiss!

Another man who was to play an important part in Pentecostal history was Pastor Gerit Polman from Amsterdam, Holland. He testified,

> 'On June 4th 1908, while in Sunderland at the Pentecostal
> Conference, I myself received the Baptism of the Holy Spirit
> while dear Pastor and Mrs. Boddy laid hands on me'.

Another key person in the early Pentecostal Movement, Stanley Frodsham, was also baptised in the Holy Spirit a few months after Wigglesworth, kneeling in the same spot, when Mary laid hands on him. He led a Pentecostal work in Bournemouth before going to America where he exerted world wide influence not only as Wigglesworth's biographer but also through his role as editor of the *Pentecostal Evangel*, the official organ of the Assemblies of God, USA.

As he went to Sunderland he prayed,

> 'Lord, I don't seem to have a prayer left in me, but wilt Thou please accept this railroad journey as a prayer three hundred miles long…[He wrote] I wended my way to the home of Brother and Sister Boddy. After an hour of fellowship I was on my knees, and looking to the Lord Jesus Christ to do for me what He did for the hundred and twenty on the Day of Pentecost…The Spirit literally fell upon me, and there was no need for anyone to tell me I had received from Him. I knew it for myself. The Lord took away my English, and I praised Him in a way I had never praised Him before, and in another tongue as the Spirit of God gave utterance'.

Mary was also instrumental in Barratt's wife, Laura, receiving the gift of tongues. In a letter that Barratt wrote to her he said, 'My dear wife, who received a mighty Baptism in London, and the 'sign' as you prayed with her in Sunderland…is going on with God'.

What a legacy this woman left the world!

A Spiritual Telegraphy

Like other Pentecostal people, Mary saw this 20th century outpouring of the Spirit in the context of the latter rain sent by God to gather in a great harvest before the end of the age.

The increase in the number of healings marked a sign of the times as the gifts of the Spirit were being restored to the church. Healing and Spirit baptism went together. Regarding tongues, this she hoped, would become 'a spiritual telegraphy to the heathen preparing for the coming of [the] King'.

The Oil Follows The Blood

After Mary was baptised in the Holy Spirit she had a vision of 'The Blood'. She explained in her testimony, 'As the Spirit spoke that word I was conscious that ALL heaven, oh, glory! (myself included) was 'worshipping the Lamb, as it had been slain'. Oh the *efficacy*, the *power* of the Blood. In one moment, what I had believed for years was illuminated as a *reality*'.

This revelation set another context for her teaching in relation to the preparation to receive the Holy Spirit. Before a seeker could be Spirit Baptised, she taught there needed to be a cleansing from sin, the blood had to be applied. She wrote, 'In the Levitical days the oil followed the blood *(Leviticus 14:17)* and this was to teach us that, in our experience the oil of the Spirit comes when the blood of Calvary is applied'. She once said with a passion, 'The mention of the blood stirs all heaven and is a poison to the hosts of hell'.

In September 1908 her booklet, *Pleading the Blood* was available and we can trace this as a foundational teaching through her writing and addresses. In effect she was saying that the conversion experience wasn't sufficient for the eradication of sin, a second blessing of sanctification was required and then the Baptism of the Holy Spirit with the accompanying sign of tongues was a third blessing. This seems almost heretical to us today but was a position held by many at the time. This theological thought prevailed throughout the early years until, as Donald Gee says, they were 'more wisely directed in the word of God'. In fact as people gave their testimonies it is evident that there was a lack of theological clarity surrounding their experiences.

A Fathomless Ocean

After her Spirit Baptism, Mary's personal life was changed. Christ lived in her and she knew it experientially not just by faith. She felt she had been 'launched into the fathomless ocean of God's love, joy and peace'. She called one of her talks, *Divine Life, Divine Love.*

Mary developed an increased sensitivity to the Holy Spirit and especially exercised the gifts of prophecy and word of knowledge. Sometimes she would express what she heard from the Lord in verses and hymns which at times were printed in *Confidence* and with her musical ability were sung from time to time.

A Rare Gift

Not just a vicar's wife busying herself with parish duties, she was thrust into the forefront of a national ministry. A busy lady indeed she spoke at conventions around the country in many major cities, sometimes alone, sometimes with her husband. More often than not she was the main speaker.

She was always well received and itinerated carrying the Pentecostal fire not in any official way but as part of a network of Spirit Baptised men and women linked together by their common experience. She ministered with many of the other 'forgotten women' as well as the 'greats' of her day. She taught her theology of Divine Healing wherever she went and she would expound her thoughts on the subject to groups of leaders thus widening her sphere of influence.

Many of her talks were published. Perhaps the longest and most sequential of her teaching was *Thoughts on a New Creation*, a sixty two page booklet which was serialised in *Confidence* from December 1909 to August 1910.

She received accolades from the known and the unknown. Carrie Judd Montgomery, another women featured in this book wrote, 'Mrs. Boddy has been wonderfully taught of God and has a rare gift of expounding His Word. Her Bible talks on Holiness and Divine Healing were very clear and powerful'. The Dutch pastor, Gerit Polman, spoke of her 'deep teaching' which has enriched and blessed him and his wife'. One report in *Confidence* began by saying, 'These notes cannot reproduce the living voice and fire of the speaker, who was carried away by the subject. This address should be pondered over sentence by sentence, and read again and again and returned to later once more'.

Ecclesiastical Intelligence

First the local, then the national press picked up what was going on in Sunderland. As always, the sensational hit the headlines.

The London Times had a column with the wonderful title 'Ecclesiastical Intelligence'. It's obvious that they had their agents infiltrating meetings at Sunderland and were reporting the actual content of what was being said rather than just some of the more extreme happenings.

Part of a talk by Mary was reported in *The Times* in May 1910, 'Mrs. Boddy in a speech declared that the church was playing with religion, but the devil was not playing; he was very busy. People were trying to get rid of sin and disease. That had been done for them at the cross. They should now prepare for glory'.

The First Sunderland Convention

Following the initial outpouring in September 1907, the Boddys hosted a conference at their church at Pentecost the following year. Called the Whitsuntide Sunderland Convention it drew together men and women from Britain and world wide who had experienced the Baptism in the Holy Spirit and spoke in tongues. By now in Britain it was estimated five hundred or so had received the blessing.

It was marked by an unusual unity. Alexander wrote, 'In our gathering of 1908 we felt that we were knit together by a love that burst all bonds of church organization and social position, and made us truly one in Christ Jesus'. It was a 20th century visual aid of *Galatians 3:28, 'There is neither Jew nor Gentile, neither slave nor free, neither male nor female, for you are all one in Christ Jesus'*. In such a setting gender divisions were swept away and Mary Boddy as well as many other women publicly exercised their God given gifts in freedom and mutuality. Mary spoke on 'No divisions and no unnecessary criticisms' and said that 'God is sweeping aside things that men have been fighting about'. Much of the conference was given up to teaching on Divine Healing and Mary's pamphlet, *Divine Health and Healing* was available for purchase. There were testimonies of healing and deliverance.

The Ministry Of Jesus

In reading the reports of the week the one thing that is striking is not the manifestations or descriptions of any wild scenes but as an observer noted, 'The one subject was Jesus glorified through the Holy Spirit'. Alexander wrote, 'They had not boasted of tongues, but had thanked God that the Lord Jesus had thus blessed them. They had lifted up Jesus and recognised Him as their Alpha and Omega'.

The Boddys had always put Jesus at the centre of their teaching and worship and believed that this was the secret of the blessing and a reason for God to be willing to use them. Mary always cautioned to get 'taken up with Jesus', not the gifts. Writing in 1909 she emphasised, 'We thank Him indeed for the gift of the Holy Ghost with the sign of tongues, but our cry is more of God'. She called her ministry, the ministry of Jesus.

Her Theme Is Always Jesus

Her first and last love was Jesus and she called worshiping Him, 'Adoring the Lamb'. She wrote, 'It is no true Baptism of the Holy Ghost which does not make us witness for Jesus'.

It's not surprising that when reporting on her meetings in Edinburgh it was written, 'Her theme is always Jesus'.

At the first Sunderland Convention Mary took her text from *John 7:38-39 (KJV), "If any man thirst, let him come to Me and drink'. This spake He of the Spirit, which they that believed in Him were to receive, for the Spirit was not yet given, because Jesus was not yet glorified'.* It was a heartfelt message that encapsulated her thinking. I believe the following extract is as relevant today as when it was delivered a hundred years ago.

> 'Are you willing to be slain, to be nothing, to drop past experiences altogether, and be occupied with Jesus only? No longer so much working for God as God working through us...Let us get down before God and glorify Jesus. We are sanctified by the offering of the body of Jesus. The death of Jesus is our death. Now, Jesus in glory is our life. The life that had overcome death comes into us.

Praise Jesus. Get Taken Up With Jesus. Crown Him Lord over all. Be filled with the Spirit and God will use you. He will bring people to us for blessing, and will flow through us to them in rivers of living water. We are only atoms in this universe, but God can do mighty things with atoms. He makes us 'sons of God".

Wow!

The Vicarage Is A Busy Place

One visitor commented, 'Though God has no leaders in this wonderful world wide outpouring of His Spirit, yet Pentecostal people the world over, look with particularly loving eyes to Sunderland and the vicar and his wife'.

It didn't all happen in the church or in the famous conventions. 'The vicarage is a busy place', one visiting PMU student wrote, 'people come with sick bodies and tired souls and all are helped'. In one article Alexander acknowledges, 'How graciously the Lord has blessed this plain little brick vicarage! He has healed many sick and baptised many in the Holy Spirit, until they call it Holy Ground'.

Not wanting to attract too much opposition, it was a smart move on Alexander's part to continue the regular services at All Saints' while the more 'Pentecostal meetings' took place in the Parish Hall, vestry or vicarage. It was in these more informal settings that Mary mainly exercised her local leadership and ministry.

Her Husband's Encouragement

Alexander Boddy believed the Word of the Lord in *Acts 2:17-18*, that God's Spirit was poured out on all people which meant that 'daughters will prophesy'. Although women generally had a subordinate place in the society of the day he operated an equal opportunities policy at least in ministry and in leadership. Without the leadership of Alexander one wonders whether women would have had such freedom in the emerging movement.

In 1911 he states in *Confidence* that only 'those that are at one with him' in regard to the ministry of women who have been baptised in the Holy Spirit (amongst other criteria) need come to the convention. These conventions were not for airing controversial points but for sharing the blessings of Pentecost.

However we have already noted that in 1914, Pastor Jonathan Paul from Berlin sought to place what he considered Scriptural limitations on the ministry of women in a debate at the Sunderland Convention called *A Woman's Place in the Church*. Alexander remained non-committal and one is left with the impression that he would be content for things to continue as they were and they did until the Pentecostal Movement became formalised as a denomination in the 1920s.

We don't read that Mary was present at this debate but her husband was advocate enough. After listening to all the varying points of view he commented, 'Where the husband and wife worked in harmony there was little or no difficulty, for they two were one'.

Unlike the Holiness women before them, these Pentecostal ladies didn't develop their own ministry apologetic and the ambiguities of the restoration of 'the Apostolic Faith' did little to help. One Pentecostal historian noted, '...taking everything in the New Testament literally gives us both daughters speaking their visions and women keeping silent'.[1]

After this debate, it doesn't seem that anything changed in Mary's ministry in fact her 'encouraging war addresses' became more authoritative. At the first Sunderland Convention Alexander had opened the session on Divine Healing by reading from *James 5:14* and endorsed his wife's ministry by saying, 'Where there are no male elders who believe, God has often raised up female elders'. Looking back at two years of revival in 1909, he said that no one gave more able help than his wife.

Her Family

All the family were involved in this move of God. Ten days after Mary was baptised in the Holy Spirit, her two daughters received the blessing when Pastor Barratt laid hands on them. Jane was fifteen and Mary (known as May) was thirteen. Jane's testimony, *The Testimony of a Vicar's Daughter* appears in an early issue of *Confidence* and they both spoke publicly of their blessing at the first Sunderland Convention.

Jane said that she shook and a power seized her tongue and jaw as she spoke in an unknown tongue and as she looked up she saw a bright light and knew it was the Lord. From this time she had a great desire to be a missionary in China. During the war both sisters were nurses, Jane in France and May in London. May Boddy went to China with the CMS as a nurse missionary in 1922.

We hear nothing about James' spiritual experiences but sadly, whilst in the Royal Flying Core during the First World War, his plane was shot down in 1918 over France and he was badly injured. One of his legs had to be amputated and he was fitted with an artificial limb. On returning to England his sister, May, nursed him for a time at St. Thomas' Hospital, London and then we find him in the 1920s married, working in the City and living in Chelsea.

They Love Them For Their Kindness

All Saints', Monkwearmouth was a working class parish and the church itself was built over a coal mine. The church still stands today but the coal mine is no longer in use. One of the first signs that something unusual was happening was a stone slab inserted in the wall of the Parish Hall which read, 'When the Fire of the Lord fell it burnt up the debt'. Even in this poor area, God had blessed them financially so they were debt free.

Following the series of meetings in September 1907 the first report in the Sunderland Echo of the meetings captured the sense of the gossip going around, 'Do you know they are holding some extraordinary services at Monkwearmouth?...Why, everybody is talking about them. Women throw themselves on the floor and then babble in unknown tongues'. The reporter comments that the meetings are the one theme of conversation in the neighbourhood.

Working class people are down to earth and would have seen through sham and hypocrisy. Alexander and Mary, although feted nationally and even internationally did not neglect parish work. Since 1886, Alexander had breathed new life into this dying parish and gaining the respect of the parishoners the Boddys had become pillars in their community.

In 1910 a student visitor from the PMU commented, 'Mr. and Mrs. Boddy are much loved by their people, and, everywhere I go in the parish I hear loving words spoken of them by the most ungodly people who love them for their kindness to them'. They remained pastors at heart.

A Spiritual War

The First World War which began in September 1914 and ended in 1918 bought changes to the parish of All Saints' as it did for all of Britain. The Parish Hall, once filled with revival scenes became a detention centre for wounded soldiers. In May 1915 Alexander made a two month trip to France to encourage the soldiers in the field while Mary kept the home fires burning. The Sunderland Conventions became a thing of the past as their location moved to Kingsway Hall in London.

In the early days of the movement, the whole context for the Pentecostal outpouring set it in the prophetic timescale of the last days. Prophesies that were given at the first Sunderland Convention regarding the soon coming of the Lord were recorded in *Confidence*. One went as far as to predict the end of the world in 1914. This apocalyptic fervour began to gain more credence as political instability grew in Europe with the threat posed by the German military machine.

Influenced by this serge of nationalism as well as a belief that Jesus was about to return, Mary's teachings began to take on a different flavour. From 1911, millennial themes emerged such as *The Coming Rapture* and *Zechariah's Horses*. She offered comfort with talks such as, *Patient Endurance* and *The Justice of God*. In 1915 she wrote a hymn called, *We're Marching on to Victory*. A title with 'double entendre', she said that the verses were given to her as in the Spirit she heard 'the marching of a victorious host'.

The Boddys took the view that it was a 'Spiritual War, a war of the Devil against Christ'. This was the Prime Minister's official line and surprisingly to our 21st century minds, the spin in the national daily papers. Throughout the war *Confidence* published articles which supported this point of view, the first being in the very first month of the war when Mary picked up on this making a study of *Revelation 6* and *Zechariah 6* to enlighten her readers scripturally and prophetically.

The Mantle Slips Away

The First World War left the nation with a wounded soul. Many men left the church, and the Pentecostal fire began to dampen. Among Pentecostal leaders there were theological divisions and an ideological gap between those whose nationalism had caused them to be ardent supporters of the war, like the Boddys and those whose pacifism had alienated them from the general mood and in some cases put them in prison.

This serves as a reminder that the Christian life is not lived in a vacuum and even a time of revival can be influenced by a culture of war. Satan will use what is at hand and the enhanced nationalism countered the flow of what God had been doing, bringing division and disunity.

The 'charismatic moment' was over and as Donald Gee put it, 'Revival enthusiasm became more sentimental than actual'. The mantle that covered Alexander and Mary slipped away and somehow the end of their lives was tinged with a sadness of what might have been. The Boddys were never interested in forming the Pentecostal Movement into a denomination and they remained members of the Church of England until the end.

In 1922, they retired to the less demanding country parish of Pittington in County Durham, still in the North East but away from the damp, biting winds and smoke that had been part of Mary's life for thirty one years. From here Alexander continued editing a bi-monthly, scaled down version of *Confidence* until 1926 and Mary still featured in its pages. For the last sixteen years of her life Mary was a semi-invalid until she died on 25th April 1928. Alexander followed his beloved wife two years later.

Alive To God In Christ Jesus

Mary Boddy is more alive to God now than she ever was while on this earth. Even though a 'forgotten woman' to many 21st century Spirit filled believers her influence was crucial in the early days of the Pentecostal Revival in Britain. She justly deserves the title 'The Mother of British Pentecostalism'.

Mary is truly alive because she has passed from this life and lives in heaven with her Lord and Saviour Jesus Christ. But she also lives through the legacy she passed on. During her life time of ministry all 'Pentecostal eyes' looked to the little parish of All Saints', Sunderland and what they did and what they taught became normative not just in Britain but world wide. Many people that had never visited the Whitsuntide Conventions or heard Mary speak at gatherings in other towns and cities had read *Confidence* and were influenced by her teachings. Indeed the Pentecostal Movement as a whole owes much of its foundational theology to this lady.

Only eternity will tell how many were baptised in the Holy Spirit under her hands and went on to do exploits for God in the power of the Spirit throughout the world. One who is truly filled with the Holy Spirit will act as a magnet. This was her secret, as she said, 'He will bring people to us for blessing and will flow through us to them in rivers of living water'. This is the ministry of Jesus.

I wonder how Mary Boddy would like to be remembered? Teacher, preacher, pastor, minister, wife, mother…co-leader of a world wide movement? I'm sure she would be delighted with the explosive ministry of Smith Wigglesworth and remember the time she laid her hands on him in her home.

But above all I believe she would want future generations to remember her as one who was *taken up with Jesus*.

---

1 Edith Blumhofer, *Restoring the Faith*, (Urbana: University of Illinois Press, 1993), 176

4

Margaret Cantel
Making Room For The Spirit

'We met in a large room of an ordinary house...
it was easy to imagine oneself in first century meetings
in Corinth or Ephesus'

Donald Gee[1]

Margaret Cantel made room for the Holy Spirit not just in her heart but by dedicating her home to the service of the Lord. For nearly thirty years her homes in Highbury became one of the 'best known and best beloved Pentecostal centres not only in London but the whole of the British Isles and far beyond'.[2]

A Young Bride

In 1907, the young bride, Margaret Cantel accompanied her husband Harry back to Britain from the States where he was the overseer of the Christian Catholic Church in England (catholic meaning universal).

It was otherwise known as a Zion Church. They were missionaries sent out from Zion City, Illinois, a literal city built by John Alexander Dowie which espoused Christian values and promoted the ministry of Healing. Dowie had visited London in 1900 and after a series of high profile meetings Harry had began a work in Upper Street, Islington preaching Holiness and Healing. Henry (Harry) Eugene Cantel was a US citizen who was born in Paris but emigrated to the States as a child. Born in 1878, Margaret had been a schoolmistress in Zion City and her father, Mr. Fielding, was one of Dowie's elders. The Cantel's Pentecostal meetings in Islington were some of the first in the country.

In 1908 the couple were publishing *The Book of Remembrance* called by Alexander Boddy 'an excellent Pentecostal paper'. Then in 1909, they changed the name to *The Overcoming Life* which was also recommended to the readers of *Confidence*. They both contained articles on Holiness from America as well as the writings of Madame Guyon which were having a significant influence in Holiness circles at that time.

Baptised In The Holy Spirit

It wasn't until his visit back home to the States in 1907 that Harry received the Baptism of the Holy Spirit and spoke in tongues. Friends noted a great spiritual change in him when he arrived back in England. We don't know when Margaret received her Baptism but we do know that it was in the vicarage at Sunderland when Mary Boddy laid hands on her. At a conference in 1916 she spoke of the blessings in her life since that day.

The work in Islington continued to grow. Harry and Margaret would often stay up until the early hours in their little rented hall helping people receive the Baptism in the Holy Spirit. As a couple they were well respected for their home life as well as their public ministry, and a hundred converts had been baptised since Harry came to these shores. The couple worked well together and theirs was a true partnership in ministry, Margaret taking responsibility for the work along with her husband. Dowie promoted the ministry of women but did insist that they marry.

Alexander Boddy, vicar of All Saints', was known to them and had visited the couple and attended their meetings. The Cantels were becoming well known and well respected in Pentecostal circles.

An Untimely Death

They were not just concerned with their own work but encouraged others by holding missions around the country. They were associated with Pentecostal pastors both at home and abroad making many friends so when on 21st August 1910, Harry died at the age of forty five, it was a great loss to the Pentecostal Movement. Harry had appendicitis which after four to five days complicated to peritonitis and proved to be fatal. It may be only conjecture but because of the Cantels' stance on 'faith' healing, it's probable that Harry refused any treatment that may have saved his life.

However, such was his standing that on the evening of his death many friends met at the Cantel home, 38 Aberdeen Road, Highbury, North London to pray for his resurrection but much as they prayed in faith for God to send his spirit back into his body it was not to be. The funeral service was held in the drawing room around the coffin.

His passing left a gap and the end of his obituary in *Confidence* reads, 'We are praying earnestly that the Lord will quickly raise up a shepherd after his own heart, who will be able to carry on the work til Jesus comes'. We don't know whether anyone was appointed to lead the work in Islington for a while but the real answer to that prayer was Margaret Cantel herself. Although she was left with a small son to care for she did not shrink back from public ministry and increasingly opened her home to visitors and for meetings. The responsibilities she had shared with Harry enabled her to carry on with the Pentecostal meetings in Upper Street.

Business As Usual

While she was married they had used their home as a 'Home of Rest'. An advertisement in *Confidence* read, 'Here invalids as well as disciples are invited to rest and seek His exceeding great and precious promises'. It was also advertised as a 'Missionary Rest Home' and was used especially for American missionaries on their way to and from foreign fields. It was a time when many missionaries were sent out from the States especially from Zion City and in those days the first or last stage in their long journey was often London. Margaret was able to offer them a 'home from home' with her American ways and cooking. She also helped with travel arrangements and shopping.

Pentecostal statesman Donald Gee[3] reminisced about a missionary meeting he once attended at her home where there was a well known American Pentecostal missionary and his party returning to India after a furlough in the States. It gives an idea of the busy place it was at number 38. He said, 'They looked rather tired as they came downstairs for the meeting. All day long Mrs. Cantel has been piloting them around the big stores in the West End making last minute purchases. The entrance hall is piled high with all their bags and trunks in readiness for the taxi cabs ordered for 6am the next morning'.

So it's no surprise that in the September 1910 edition of *Confidence*, on the page after her husband's obituary, we read, 'Our dear Sister, Mrs. H.E. Cantel will continue to keep on the home at 38 Aberdeen Road, Highbury (N. London) and will gladly welcome visitors as before. Those who sympathise with her will, for the sake of her dear husband, make this known and so encourage her at this time'. *Confidence* the following year reported, 'Mrs. Cantel still continues the meetings as in Pastor Cantel's time…the Lord is with them there'.

It has been said that one of the first Pentecostal weddings in England was held at her home when Alice Rowlands and Stanley Frodisham (later to become a leader in the American Assemblies of God) were united by Smith Wigglesworth in 1911.

Gee said of this remarkable lady who he recognised as an 'outstanding Christian', 'She possessed all the vivid charm of her nationality, coupled with strong faith, business ability and fervent spirituality'. The main work of her life was just beginning.

A Step Of Faith

When Harry died Margaret was left in a foreign country with no visible means of support yet she stayed to continue the work they had started as a couple. In September 1912, two years after her husband's death, Margaret took a step of faith and moved to a larger home at 73 Highbury New Park, North London to continue her ministry. It was called *Maranatha*, an ancient Hebrew word meaning 'The Lord is coming soon,' or 'Oh, Lord, come soon'. This was a word used by the early Christians and certainly expressed current Pentecostal expectation.

Large enough to incorporate the assembly in Islington, *Maranatha* also provided comfortable guest accommodation and a meeting room. She assumed full financial responsibility for the house and although some wealthy members of the PMU (The Pentecostal Missionary Union) stood as guarantors they were never needed. It was to her credit that they realised the important contribution she was making to missionary work and were willing to support her in this way. Charges to guests were always on a voluntary basis and if finances were short then they prayed and believed together for the Lord to supply the needs. And He did!

Donald Gee comments that this generosity of spirit contributed to the spiritual atmosphere that made *Maranatha* a place of blessing.

Dedicated To The Lord

Maranatha was dedicated to the Lord on 2nd October 1912. It is described in *Confidence* as an up-to-date house in a quiet respectable part of the city. Because of its privacy it was suited for informal gatherings and prolonged times of waiting on the Lord in prayer.

Friends gathered that afternoon and it shows the respect with which Margaret was held when we read of the calibre of men who were present. Among them were the 'Apostle of Faith', Smith Wigglesworth, Mr. Mundell of the PMU and Pastor T.M. Jeffreys, a leader of the Pentecostal work in Wales.

We read in *Confidence*, 'Mrs. Cantel gave a touching description of the Lord's fidelity towards her and the way she had been clearly and unmistakably led to remove from 38 Aberdeen Road, Highbury to the present address. Her remarks were followed by Mr. Wigglesworth and Pastor Jeffreys whose addresses were spiritually helpful and fraught with blessing for all, as they dedicated the home and our sister to the work of the Lord. After a season of prayer the meeting closed and the friends partook of tea and then inspected the home'.

The home was highly recommended by Alexander to any friends visiting London for conventions, realising that 'by such visits our sister will be enabled to maintain for God's glory the work which he has entrusted her'. In other words it became a source of income for this young widow.

The Blessing Continues

Every now and again there were short reports of the meetings at her home that appeared in editions of *Confidence*. 'All night prayer meetings were held last month at *Maranatha*. About forty five were present' (December 1913). '*Maranatha* continues to be a haven of rest for Pentecostal travellers and others and we hear of much blessing in the meetings held there' (December 1914).

Smith Wigglesworth was a frequent visitor as was A.S. Booth Clibborn, the grandson of William and Catherine Booth of the Salvation Army. Welsh revivalists stayed there while holding meetings in London in 1913 and there were often Scandinavians who had come to learn English. Cecil Polhill, president and director of the PMU regularly attended the prayer gatherings.

Young men from The Pentecostal Missionary Training Home would arrive on special nights to hear missionaries speak of their work in countries around the world. It became a busy place indeed.

At first Margaret had to furnish her new home with the furniture from her previous house and it appeared rather sparse as she spread it around. The meetings took place in what was supposed to be the drawing room with texts from the Bible around the wall. Donald

Gee, a frequent visitor from 1913 onwards recalls, 'Of course there was a little table for the leader of the meetings; a small organ was placed diagonally across one corner; there were strips of old stair carpet on the floor, and an odd collection of chairs augmented from all the bedrooms on crowded occasions'. As the work grew under the blessing of God so did the furnishings.

There was a steady stream of missionaries and leaders who stayed at her home and so there was 'a constant supply of stirring testimony and gifted ministry'. Margaret often led the meetings and played the organ. Sometimes, on special nights, the numbers were such that the door of the room was left open and the stair case acted as overflow seating.

New Testament Days

Donald Gee who later became the Chairman of the Assemblies of God for Great Britain and Ireland and a respected world wide leader was taken to a night of prayer rather unwillingly by his mother to what he affectionately called 'Highbury' in 1913. In his own words, he was, 'captivated by the sense of God's presence'. It was after being challenged by an old preacher in Margaret's house that same year that he knelt by his bed at home and was filled with the Holy Spirit. It was at 'Highbury' that he preached his first sermon and was influenced by many contemporary and future Pentecostal leaders.

In *Wind and Flame*, his history of the Pentecostal Movement, he gives an insight into those meetings which he says, 'had a unique thrill because they were anchored in the New Testament'. He writes of his first taste of a Pentecostal meeting at Margaret's home.

'A company of fifty get on their knees for a prolonged period of prayer. Strips of well worn carpet slightly soften the bare boards... After an hour or more of a rising and falling wave of audible prayer and worship, in which all take part quite freely and spontaneously, sometimes individually, sometimes collectively, the young man [speaking of himself] whispers to his mother, 'These people pray as though God were in the room,' 'So He is,' she replies and goes on praying silently'.

He writes of a missionary meeting he attended at 'Highbury',

> 'The missionary begins to speak; all tiredness vanishes;
> the meeting is gripped: The Acts of the Apostles seems to
> come to life again from the pages of the New Testament.
> Is this Barnabas or Titus that we are listening to again? Is
> this London? Or is it Antioch or Corinth? The centuries are
> forgotten. We are feeling the power of the Eternal Spirit.
> Someone is speaking in an unknown tongue, another
> interprets. Our hearts are reverently bowed. Our hearts tell
> us that God himself has spoken'.

One thing that made an impression on this young man was the
egalitarian nature of the proceedings. This was a hallmark of the
early days of the Pentecostal Movement where barriers of class,
gender and race were broken down as we read of in *Galatians 3: 28,
'There is neither Jew or Gentile, neither slave nor free, neither male
nor female, for you are all one in Christ Jesus'*. On his first occasion
at 'Highbury', Gee saw the PMU's Cecil Polhill, the wealthy Squire
of Howbury Hall, Bedford, who was leading the meeting, share
his hymn book with one of the house maids. In the class conscious
society of the day this was something to be remarked on.

Such meetings made a great impression on Donald Gee and it
is thanks to Margaret's faith and obedience to God that she was
instrumental in the life of a young man's journey with the Lord who
went on to have such an influence on many people. She was a woman
who facilitated this new move of the Spirit of God which touched so
many more lives than we will ever know.

A Woman Of Influence

Margaret's ministry was not just confined to meetings in her home. In
June 1916 she was a speaker at the National Pentecostal Convention at
Westminster. She shared the platform with such leaders as Alexander
and Mary Boddy from Sunderland, Smith Wigglesworth, Cecil Polhill,
Eleanor Crisp, the Principal of the PMU Ladies' Training Home, Lydia
Walshaw, a Pentecostal leader from Halifax and Catherine Price who
also opened her home for prayer meetings in London. Many other
friends from the Sunderland Conventions were there too.

As well of speaking of the many blessings in her life since being filled with the Holy Spirit she spoke of 'the happy times' they have in their home at '73'.

Margaret exercised considerable influence in the early days of the Pentecostal Movement. In 1924 she was the only woman among a group of fifteen who met in Birmingham to prepare a constitution for the formation of the first Pentecostal denomination in Britain, the Assemblies of God. Then later that year in May there was a consolidatory conference held at her house in Highbury to put the final touches to the constitution and for it to gain general approval. From this beginning the Assemblies of God began in 1924 with seventy four assemblies.

'Highbury' bought together two Pentecostal streams. George Jeffreys of the Elim Pentecostal Churches and Donald Gee of the Assemblies of God were both frequent visitors. Yet even though there was a spiritual unity, because of differences in church structure they remained as separate denominations.

Her Passing

Like her husband, Margaret went to be with the Lord at an early age. She was forty eight. We don't know what she died of but after being confined to her bed for five days 'she just fell asleep' and suffered no pain.

Room In Heart And Home

How different things would have been if as a newly bereaved young woman she had packed her bags and returned to Zion City. But she had made room for God in her heart and He was able to not only comfort her but encourage her to continue the work they had started as a couple.

Hospitality was a gift she excelled in. She made room for God in her heart and room for God in her home. No wonder Gee says that the meetings he went to reminded him of early Christianity.

In the New Testament we read of women who had churches in their houses. In Laodicea, Nympha had a church which met in her home *(Colossians 4:15)*. Many gathered at Mary's house to pray for Peter's release when he was imprisoned *(Acts 12:12)*. Chloe headed a household in Corinth *(1 Corinthians 1:11)* and it's probable that a church met in Phoebe's home in Cenchrea *(Romans 16:1-2)*. Appia, who Paul calls 'our sister' was also a leader of a house church in Colossae. Lydia *(Acts 16:13-15)*, Paul's first convert to the Christian faith in Europe invited him and his companions to stay at her home in Philippi after the whole household had been baptised. As she opened up her home and her heart it's reasonable to assume that they were the first of many to take advantage of her hospitality. Not only did women play a prominent role in establishing these house churches but participated in leadership and ministry. So Margaret had a firm precedent for what she did in allowing her home to be used for 'church' as believers gathered together.

Our 21ˢᵗ century social structure is so different from that of the first century where households extended to include not just relatives but servants and slaves. Yet the principle is the same. Our homes are gifts from the Lord and can be stewarded for His purposes. We don't have to run official 'Homes of Rest', yet we can bless all those who enter our households in a myriad of different ways. We can have 'church' in our homes whether a formal or informal gathering and *practice hospitality (Romans 12:13)* as we are so often encouraged to do so by writers of the New Testament.

The story of Margaret Cantel tells of a women who was raised up to bless many by embracing responsibility following the death of her husband and by opening her home. She was a single mother with a young child with no visible means of support at a time when there was no social security to ease the way yet had her ear attuned to how God could use her.

I'm sure that as a young school mistress in America she would never have dreamed that her life would have such an impact on a generation flowing in a new wave of the Spirit which would sweep the globe.

Such is the impact of one life lived before God who purposed to 'make room for the Spirit'.

---

1 Donald Gee, *These Men I Knew,* (Nottingham: AOG Publishing House, 1980), 33

2 Donald Gee, *These Men I Knew,* (Nottingham: AOG Publishing House, 1980), 31

3 For this and other reminisces see Donald Gee, *Wind and Flame,* (Croydon: AOG Publishing House, 1967), Chapter VII

5

Lydia Walshaw
Down To Earth Spirituality

*'In the kitchen that is where the Power of Holiness must
be seen and felt. Most of us will have to go back from this
lovely place [Kingsway Hall in London] into kitchens and
workshops and busy places of life'*

Lydia Walshaw

Lydia A. Walshaw was a remarkable woman of spiritual insight and
integrity which expressed itself in a down to earth manner whether
she was speaking at a convention or involved in the practicalities of
leading her group of missionary intercessors. She emerged in the
early years of the Pentecostal Movement and remained involved in
some way or another until she was well into her nineties.

A Fire Kindled Within

We read a testimony given by an unknown lady at the 1911 Sunderland Convention who claims to be the first lady in Halifax to speak in tongues. Although not named as Lydia, I suspect it was since it is characteristic of the way she spoke, mentions a mission room and it certainly made an impression on the assembled gathering. This is how it was reported in *Confidence*.

> 'She was praying alone in a mission room when she felt her cheeks shake and her lips quiver and soon she was speaking and singing in tongues. The Lord had graciously blessed her. She had been speaking in tongues frequently ever since. She said it seemed that a fire was then kindled in her. It was usually small but sometimes it was very big. She never talked about her neighbours now. At one time there were certain people she could not love, but now she loved everybody. She could throw her arms around and kiss them in all their dirt and sin.
>
> The lady from Halifax concluded her striking address, which elicited many calls of 'Hallelujah' from the gathering, by singing in a rich, full voice one of the hymns she said the Lord had given her. It was a hymn of faith rendered without instrumental accompaniment, in a way that had a great effect upon the listeners'.

At The Beginning

Lydia Walshaw was in at the beginning of the Pentecostal Movement in Britain. At the first Sunderland Convention in June 1908 we read in *Confidence* that she participated in a discussion that took place on the first day. It was on 'waiting meetings', those times that were set aside for prayer for those who wished to be baptised in the Holy Spirit. To be involved in such a discussion reveals how well respected she was and even in the early years of the movement had some experience in dealing in such matters.

A Public Role

Lydia was born in America in 1854 although she was British by nationality. Married to Yorkshire born Joseph, the couple had a son, Saxon, in 1882. In a photograph taken in 1921 of a group of delegates at the International Pentecostal Conference in Amsterdam we also see her grandson aged around ten or eleven sitting at her husband's feet. Joseph was a respected solicitor and the couple lived in Halifax, Yorkshire in the north of England. Her husband's profession would have guaranteed them a place among burgeoning middle classes and altholugh she had a maid seemed to remain thoroughly down to earth. In 1914 their address was Bell Grove, Rothwell Road, Halifax. A house that is recognised by a name rather than a number is a sure sign of being comfortably off.

However, it was Lydia who took the more public role often accompanied by her husband who sat with her on the platform. Joseph had a striking appearance with a long flowing white beard and a ruddy complexion while Lydia looked prim and was usually dressed in navy blue with a small 'holiness' bonnet with a bow under the chin. An impressive couple.

Emmaus

She didn't lead a church but had formed a group called Emmaus who were missionary intercessors. These Sunday morning prayer meetings were in held in her home and began as far back as 1885. They were not advertised but Lydia believed that the Lord would send the right people to her. About thirty turned up to the first meeting. The only clue as to what was happening behind the front door was a small engraved sign, *Emmaus*, on the gate.

Emmaus continued as a missionary prayer group and Lydia had no interest in formalising it into a 'church'. Later on this work in Halifax was to become part of the Elim Pentecostal denomination.

She influenced many who were associated with Emmaus, one of whom was the now deceased, veteran missionary Harold Womersley who went to work with the Congo Evangelistic Mission in 1924. Many too were sent out from Emmaus to speak in other chapels and churches nearer home.

As Donald Gee[1] says, 'Her 'boys' were always her old friends...Men and women, young and old alike were happy to talk with 'Granny Walshaw' as she came to be affectionately called by a new generation'.

Keeping The Testimony Real

Prayer and missions were her passion and she was a welcome and acceptable speaker at Pentecostal conventions all over the country. In *Confidence* we read of her speaking at Sunderland, London, Bradford and Edinburgh to name just a few places.

The sermons she gave always centred around these subjects and were immensely challenging. They give us an insight into her character because of the personal and homely illustrations she used. Pentecostal leader Donald Gee knew her personally and was obviously fond of her. He said that she helped to keep the Pentecostal testimony real when some of the men speakers were in danger of becoming super-spiritual.

He tells the story where they shared a platform at a convention in London where he was playing the piano at one end. On the platform were what he called 'a collection of dry reverends' so she shifted her chair next to his in order, as she said, 'to keep each other warm'. Such was the dry humour and reality of this lady who had made Yorkshire her home.

Halifax Conventions

As the work grew she began to hold conventions where larger premises were needed. These were begun as early as November 1909 and they attracted high profile speakers such as Mary Boddy. It is interesting to note that these were not women's conferences yet at this particular one all the speakers were women. It lasted three days and if the report in *Confidence* is anything to go by it was a great success, although it was written by our Lydia!

When Smith Wigglesworth stopped his annual Easter conventions in Bradford in 1924 she continued them under the banner of Emmaus. She comments in her particular way, 'All the meetings were well attended, there were no regrettable occurrences; all the helpers were in their places and did their work like well oiled machinery, without a squeak, and the radiant joy of the Lord shining on their faces'.

Dry Their Tears And Make Them Smile

The group at Emmaus did not just pray but they gave. Their annual balance sheet eventually exceeded four figures and that was at a time when the average weekly wage was often as little as £1. This was due to the influence of Lydia whose heart we can hear in this extract from a message she gave at the London Convention in 1920 entitled, *The Joy of Giving* which was printed in *Confidence*.

'I believe in tithing, I believe in free will offerings, I believe in thank offerings, I believe in all the privileges of giving. You have the joy of pouring all out at His feet. I see to it that He shall have all He entrusted to me. I can afford all He tells me to do. Had we done it we should have such a plenty. Here are missionaries wanting to go out; there are those on the field suffering, suffering. Have we taken it to heart, we who are at home? Our money is the Lord's and it is a great privilege to give...

We in Halifax have missionary meetings once a week and have extra ones...There is hardly any country where we haven't got a finger in the pie. What a delight it is to say we've got so and so there. One says, 'My heart has been weeping before the Lord for the Armenians; let's send them something to dry their tears and make them smile'. And while we are drying their tears we are drying our own tears...We are going to pray that we who stay by the stuff may help to sustain those on the battlefield'.

At the 1917 Whitsuntide Convention at Kingsway Hall she challenged Pentecostal leaders to support the missionary effort. She had said she was in touch with seventy three missionary societies and that Emmaus gave £500 the previous year to foreign missions. These were sacrificial contributions – mostly the gifts of working people.

Alexander Boddy who was present said that after her address there was a great humbling in prayer by the leaders who acknowledged how poor their efforts had been for foreign missions. Lydia's passion for mission certainly helped keep the cause high on the agenda.

Be Intelligent Shareholders

Much of the money that was raised went to support missionaries who were sent out by the Pentecostal Missionary Union (PMU) which had been formed in 1908. Lydia used to be there at the annual missionary meetings encouraging them to give and pray.

In 1916 we read in *Confidence* that she appealed to all present to become shareholders in the blessed PMU work. She said, 'You must put something in, if you wish to reap dividends in heaven. Be intelligent shareholders'.

She encouraged them to continue in prayer with this little story,

'She knew one who had a vision of prayers going up in the form of little clouds. Different ones in the prayer meeting sent up those clouds. There was one whose cloud seemed to be very weak and it could not get up and it came down again. An earnest sister knelt beside and joined her and prayed with her and her little cloud grew strong and went up again and now it reached the throne. Union in prayer brings wonderful results'.

So Few Lovers

She often spoke on prayer at other conventions. *The Life of Prayer* was her subject at the 1912 Sunderland Convention when 'she touched all hearts with the fragrance of her message'. She gave this illustration.

'A brother in the Lord had once said to her that when he married his wife he married her for companionship and true love; he did not marry her so she may wash the dishes. But, she said, 'When there is true love how the washing of dishes, or any necessary work, becomes easy for love's sake. The Lord loves to see our faces turned up to him, and uttering a prayer He has placed there Himself, for Himself and to Himself'.

She then said a statement is as true today as it was then, 'There are many workers for the Lord but so few lovers'.

A Passion For Intercession

Her passion for intercession and her desire to see all Christians rising to the challenge and moving situations by prayer can be seen in this extract from a message she gave in 1924.

> 'I believe we have yet to learn what it would be with a Pentecostal Church in England that truly understood the work of intercession. I believe God the Holy Ghost wants to teach us that it is not only the people on the platform who can move things by prayer. You people, the Lord can move things through you. We have to learn the breath of the Holy Ghost. He will formulate words that come into your hearts'.

That Does Very Nicely

Lydia was not a theologian nor was she well educated in the accepted sense of the word. She said that she had not found it easy to learn at school and had suffered. In those days teachers didn't like to be questioned so Lydia had to listen and make the best of it. She said, 'My blessed Lord helps me understands things…I don't know anything about theology but I know what He means, and that does very nicely'.

She carried a well worn Bible whose pages carried a familiarity which helped her find the references she wanted. Not remembering the chapter and verse, the quotes she wanted were just 'there' on a certain page.

The Common Life Of Holiness

She gained spiritual wisdom from the Lord in her everyday life. There was no duality in her living, no holy days or holy places. Lydia believed a life of holiness was lived before the Lord twenty four hours a day seven days a week. Holiness was an issue of the heart that was lived out in real situations not just in meetings.

At the London Convention in June 1916 she spoke on *The Common Life of Holiness.*

> 'I know a great deal of the trivial round and common task – a very common task, and the Lord teaches me in such a way as to enable me to understand the answers. He gives me my requests. He teaches me all the way along in my everyday life. This is what I feel we need in this revival of Holiness, something that is holy not merely in a meeting, but something that is holy all the days of the week, all the year round, under all circumstances and conditions. *A Revival of Holiness.*
>
> I remember once writing out a little text and my old maid who has been with me for many years – the text was in connection with 'Holiness unto the Lord', said, 'Where shall we put this up in this house?' I said, 'Let us hang it over the broomstick; I think that is the best place to have it. We will stick it up in the kitchen; I think it will do very well in the place where folk are looking at us'. In the kitchen that is where the Power of Holiness must be seen and felt. Most of us will have to go back from this lovely place into kitchens and workshops and busy places of life'.

Glory To God For The Kitchen

She had the knack of using every day illustrations to hammer home her point and she did so most effectively.

In one message she was talking about how to get peace in our lives. 'Get right with Him and then submit yourself so thoroughly to Him that He can work His righteousness through you to others and the peace will come'. She illustrated this by talking about making starch.

> 'One day I was making some starch and you know you go on pouring the water until it comes. What do you mean? Folks who make starch know what I mean. And when 'it comes' it is the right consistency and is right for the purpose for which we want it – it is just right. Hallelujah for the kitchen! I am so much obliged to God for the kitchen. Glory to God for the kitchen!'

If Sugar's Going Up, I'm Going Up!

Rising prices didn't faze her. I'm sure the men in the congregation used to smile as they heard her talk about price rises of sugar and coal. But she always turned things around to a spiritual point. This following extract is from a talk she gave at the 1920 London Convention hitting home the truth that *'The Lord is the Possessor of Heaven and Earth' (Genesis 14:19 KJV)*.

'Everything in the earth is the Lords. If you believe that you haven't got anything. 'My money, my house, my furniture'. You haven't got any money, house, furniture; these are only ours as we are stewards of these things.

Some people are always walking around poor. They measure their possessions by what they have in their pockets by what they have in the bank. I am not poor; I am exceedingly rich. I am a multi millionaire. The silver and gold are the Lord's and I am a child of the King. I can go to Him for what I want. It isn't what I've got in my pocket, it's what I can fetch out for other people. We are just as rich as we are prayerful. You can have a good time if you believe He means just what He says. Praise God for all things. Give thanks at all times.

Someone says, 'What are we going to do if things go up like this?' Why? Are we going to pay for them? Coal at 40/- a ton! Praise God what is there to grumble at? Sugar 2/- a lb. Well give thanks to God! Margarine! Well it agreed with me better than butter. Someone said, 'I never heard such a thing in my life. What an idea!' We can always praise God for what we like but how about when we get what we don't like? Praise God still. 'But how can we if things keep going up? We will pay for them but where's the money going to come from?' I will pay out of the Lord's pocket.

If you get that revelation in your soul, that He is the possessor of heaven and earth, it will make all the difference in your life. If sugar is going up. I am going up. It is another sign. Lord I shall be going up directly. Let them be signs for us, for that is what they are. If you have eyes to see and hearts to believe they are all signs.'

A message on giving, prosperity and eschatology rolled into one!

A Lump Of Holiness

The way she expressed spiritual truths was unique to her personality. In a message on Holiness she said,

> 'Holiness is not a thing for which you go to God and say, 'Please give me holiness in a lump' and you expect it will all come down and you will swallow it whole, and you will be holy forever. It is not like that a bit. God is holy and I understand that holiness is the life of God imparted to me as I open myself to God and let the blood of Jesus cleanse me, and let the Lord work in my heart'.

Her down to earth forthright manner comes across in another extract from *The Joy of Giving*. 'I talk to my soul. If my soul gets discouraged I take it out and put it down in front of me and talk to it. 'Why are you discouraged? What is the matter with you?'' Another time she got down on her hands and knees on the platform and lapped water with her hands to illustrate the story of how Gideon chose his army. One can imagine the audience laughing affectionately at this woman of God.

A Day Of The Holy Ghost

She was a woman who moved in the power of God. The Holy Spirit who filled her being gave her a great boldness. She said in 1924,

> 'This has been a day in the Holy Ghost. The last three months have been the greatest days of my life...I have seen greater things than I ever expected to see and I am more hungry to see greater things yet. The great thing at conventions is to get us immersed in God that we may see signs and wonders in the name of the Lord Jesus'.

The following extracts are from the same talk and show that she actually moved in what she taught and believed. She told a story of how she had ministered healing.

> 'I was taken to see a young woman who was very ill. The young man who showed me the way said, 'I am afraid we shall not be able to do much here, because of her mother and the doctors are coming'. I said, 'This is what God had

bought me here for', and when I prayed the young woman was instantly healed by the power of God. God the Holy Ghost stays in our hearts today and it is only He who can do it. After that we got crowds, and I ministered to the sick among them for two hours. The secret for the future is living and moving in the power of the Holy Ghost'.

Whist travelling through Switzerland she must have surprised these three men with her boldness. She says,

'When I was in a little room at Bern waiting for my passport, I found a lot of people but I couldn't speak to them, so I got hold of three men and pulled them to me. They stared but I got them to their knees. Then we prayed and the revival began. I couldn't talk to them but I could show them the way to talk to someone else'.

Mr. Joseph Walshaw

Although Joseph Walshaw sometimes appeared on platforms with his wife, it was she who exercised the more prominent public role of preaching, teaching and leadership. Her gift did indeed make room for her. However not all Pentecostal leaders were happy with the way women were having such freedom in ministry and so there was the discussion at the 1914 Sunderland Convention on the subject of *A Woman's Place in the Church*. In the report of this we read that Joseph took part and made a comment which is interesting bearing in mind the activities of his wife.

He was at pains to point out that *1 Timothy 2:12-15* had nothing to do with teaching in the church but only referred to domestic life because of the reference to child bearing, thus in his opinion freeing his wife scripturally to teach.

Perhaps sensing the awkward position Joseph was in Alexander steered the discussion suggesting that perhaps the distinction between home and church was not so clear cut since Christians can be a small group gathered in a home or as a larger church group. I wonder what Lydia would have said had she been present.

Spanning A Century

Lydia went home to be with her Lord on 9th February 1951. She had lived to the ripe old age of ninety seven and outlived her husband who died at ninety four in 1945. Born at the time of 19th Century revivalism, her life spanned a century of immense change which included two world wars and saw Pentecostalism solidify as a denomination and Christianity itself become marginalised.

Faith By Itself…Is Dead

So we read of another life lived several generations ago yet which still speaks. Lydia Walshaw was a woman whose feet were firmly on this earth while her eyes were on heaven. She was a passionate intercessor but it was a passion that led to action and good works exemplified by her faithful fund raising for missionaries. I'm sure that she would have agreed with this very practical scripture we read in the book of James,

> 'Suppose a brother or sister is without clothes or daily food. If one of you says to him, 'Go, in peace; keep warm and well fed,' but does nothing about their physical needs, what good is it? In the same way, faith by itself, if it not accompanied by action, is dead' (James 2:15-17).

She was a lover of God and a lover of people with an understanding that real Christianity must be lived out in the real world not just in conventions and conferences, such was her 'down to earth spirituality'.

When Jesus stood in the synagogue in Nazareth He set out the purpose of His mission,

> 'The Spirit of the Lord is on Me, because He has anointed Me to preach good news to the poor. He has sent Me to proclaim freedom for the prisoners and recovery of sight to the blind, to set the oppressed free, to proclaim the year of the Lord's Favour' (Luke 4:18-19).

The Gospel is good news for the whole of a person's life not just a ticket to heaven. I think Lydia Walshaw had got hold of that. Her views displayed a 'kingdom mentality' and although she probably wouldn't have expressed it in those terms she certainly believed in the power of the Gospel needed to work in the 'kitchens and workshops and busy places of life'.

Because of their longevity, Lydia and Joseph became a spiritual mother and father to the Pentecostal Movement. Donald Gee said of Lydia Walshaw, '[She] was one of those personalities that seem to flourish in the early years of a revival movement before it has had time to solidify into a denomination'. What an insightful comment. She was a lady who, unfettered by institutionalism, was free to be just what God had made her to be, her Yorkshire wit and wisdom shining through a godly character.

---

1 For Gee's comments see Donald Gee, *These Men I Knew,* (Nottingham: AOG Publishing House, 1980), 84-86

6

Carrie Judd Montgomery Faith And Healing Homes

'The only thing that counts is faith expressing itself through love'

Galatians 5:6

Before Carrie Judd Montgomery was known in British Pentecostal circles she already had a well established ministry in the United States of America. She was a speaker and teacher who was said to be the first woman to itinerate across America. She wrote extensively, established and directed faith and healing homes, was involved in social work and for sixty six years edited *Triumphs of Faith*, subtitled *A monthly journal devoted to faith healing and to the promotion of Christian Holiness*. Carrie was a remarkably gifted religious entrepreneur who after being a minister for over forty years joined the American Assemblies of God in 1917.

This experienced, capable and godly woman found her place in the hearts of the early British Pentecostals and her influence extended in a number of significant areas. For these reasons she deserves to be among those at 'the source of the river'.

The Honoured Editress

Alexander Boddy was a reader of *Triumphs of Faith* and referred to her in the August 1908 issue of *Confidence* as 'the honoured editress...well known in religious circles in the USA'. Following her Baptism in the Holy Spirit in June 1908 she wrote about her experience in *Triumphs*.

Up to this time she had remained sceptical and had not advocated 'Pentecost with signs' but now having joined the ranks of those who spoke in tongues Alexander was able to say 'May the Lord use her mightily in the days that are before her'. Ever alert to keep his readers up to date with moves of the Spirit, he contacted Carrie and printed her testimony in November's *Confidence*.

From this time on, Carrie's writings appeared regularly in *Confidence*. She and her husband visited the Sunderland and London Conventions in 1909 and Alexander returned two visits to the States one in 1912 where he visited their *Home of Peace* in California and the other to minister at a camp meeting in Cazadero which he had to cut short because of the outbreak of the First World War in 1914.

A Woman With A Testimony

Carrie was a woman with a testimony. Like all Pentecostals it was important that she tell the story of how she had received the Baptism of the Spirit. It was her badge of credibility. Carrie had also been dramatically healed in 1879 after being an invalid for two years and near to death. A year later, her book, *The Prayer of Faith* which gave details of her healing and theology gained international recognition and thrust her into the forefront of the Healing Movement at the age of twenty two. It is because she was such a gifted writer we know so much more about her life than many of the other women featured in this book.

The Promise Of The Father

The Promise of the Father was the title she used for her testimony as it appeared in *Triumphs* and later in *Confidence*. Like many Holiness teachers, she believed that she had already received the Baptism of the Holy Spirit as a second work of sanctification. When she was healed she had an experience of the Holy Spirit which revealed Jesus to her in a new way and from that time on she says that 'a power to testify came into [her] soul'. New truths were revealed to her in the Word of God and from that time her teaching ministry became very influential.

After the outpouring of the Holy Spirit at the Azusa Street Mission she watched the Pentecostal work 'carefully and prayerfully'. There were things that did not appeal to the calm, steady nature of this Episcopalian lady such as the wild meetings which she thought bore the hallmark of confusion, fleshly excess and unscriptural use of the gifts. Her husband had been warned not to go there because of the 'wild fire' but he went and heard as he said, 'heavenly voices' which caused him to seek after the blessing for himself.

Always hungering for more of God, Carrie saw some of her personal friends who were of her persuasion and conviction speak in tongues and she began to 'thirst for the fullness'. What impressed Carrie most was the increased love and humility in their lives rather than the gifts. Seeking for the fullness of the Spirit in her life did not negate any of her previous experiences but she believed they were just a foretaste of what she saw as God's best, the 'full Baptism'.

Streams Become Rivers

During the summer of 1908 Carrie travelled to the east of America and knew that in comparison to the 'rivers of the Spirit' that her friends were experiencing, she only had 'streams'. In her testimony she describes in detail the experience of the power of the Spirit she felt as friends prayed for her and then on June 29th 1908, one week later in the home of an old friend in Chicago she received the fullness she had been seeking. Her testimony in *Confidence* relates the experience.

'In a few moments I uttered a few scattered words in an unknown tongue, and then burst into a language that came pouring out in great fluency and clearness. The brain seemed entirely passive, the words not coming from that source at all, but from an irresistible volume of power within, which seemed to possess my whole being, spirit, soul and body. For nearly two hours I spoke and sang in unknown tongues. I was filled with joy and praise to God with an inward depth of satisfaction in Him which cannot be described...The rivers of living water flowed through me and divine ecstasy filled my soul'.

Claimed By Faith

Ever wary of manifestations, she notes that in her experience, 'There was no shaking and no contortions of the body' but she did become physically weak and staggered across the floor. As we would say today she was 'drunk in the Spirit'.

Several times in her testimony she refers to this experience as being claimed by faith, a position she held to unswervingly whether it be praying for the Baptism in the Spirit or healing. She wrote, 'He keeps me continually standing by faith in His finished work, not walking by sight, and this is my answer to those who might accuse me of depending on manifestations in my Christian life'.

A Year With The Comforter

One year after her testimony appeared in *Confidence* Alexander printed the contents of a booklet that Carrie made available through *Triumphs of Faith* called *A Year with the Comforter*. Whilst seeking the Baptism of the Spirit for herself, it was the fruit in people's lives that impressed her so it's not surprising that she looks to the fruit in her own life and 'gives a little testimony' as to what the past year of walking with God had meant.

In the context of asking the Lord for rain in the time of the latter rain *(Zechariah 10:1)* she notes the increase in her life of holy joy, holy stillness, love, power to witness, teachableness, love for the Word of God and an increased spirit of praise and worship. She tells of a new realization of her 'own nothingness' and of the 'treasure' she has within.

Be Still And Know

This is a woman who knew God and although she speaks of a year of 'being increased in utterance' she realised that there is a place of stillness which transcends this experience. She described this eloquently and it is a place which is at the core of her spirituality.

> 'But I would also add that there have been times of communion, of feasting beneath His shadow, drinking within His banqueting house, abiding in the sacred stillness of the secret of His presence, times too sacred to attempt to describe even to those who are nearest and dearest, when even tongues have ceased, and neither in English nor in any other tongue has it been possible to find expression. With no language but the heavenly rapture of our adoring spirit…could we then look up into His blessed face, as all our being was hushed by His sweet command, 'Be still and know that I am God'. And in His own unspeakable stillness our whole being drank in His love and power, and knew Him as our Lord and our God'.

A Godly Home

Born in 1858, Carrie came from a godly home and made a commitment to follow the Lord at the age of eleven. Her spiritual formation was nurtured in the family setting and she traced an increased blessing on her life back to her confirmation in the Episcopalian Church.

She later wrote, 'I learnt the vital points of the Bible very clearly. When I was a child, I used to watch my mother very closely in our pew to see if she really believed the prayers that came from her lips. If she told us she prayed about anything, I used to watch if her prayers were answered, and when they were my faith increased'. She cautioned, 'Mother, your children are looking at you'.

Walk By Faith

Many of the women who were prominent in the early Pentecostal Movement could testify to divine healing. In Carrie's case this was a remarkable event that was to change the course of her whole life. Never a strong young women, she suffered a spinal fever after a fall which left her a helpless invalid. After two years of pain and a deterioration of her physical condition, she was not expected to live.

It was at this point when Carrie's father heard of a black lady, Elizabeth Mix, who had a healing ministry. Through correspondence she promised to pray for the young girl at an appointed hour and told her that no matter 'how you feel get right out of bed and begin to walk by faith. Strength will come, disease will depart and you will be made whole'.

The miracle happened as prophesied and in 1879, at the age of twenty one Carrie got out of bed unaided. Within an hour strength entered her body, her pallid complexion began to change and she was able to eat and drink as those with her stood astonished.

News of this miracle spread, the first account being published in the local paper of the Judd's home town, Buffalo, New York. Other papers picked up the story and it even found its way into the British press.

The Prayer Of Faith

Always a gifted writer, she used her talents to write her first book which was published in 1880. Entitled *The Prayer of Faith*, it recounted the miracle that had occurred in her life. At this time Divine Healing was called 'a faith cure' and she used the book to explain how to pray and believe for God to intervene in a person's life in miracles and healings. Elizabeth Mix had encouraged her with a scripture from *James 5:15 (KJV) 'The prayer of faith shall save the sick'* which proved to be a foundational scripture for her life's work.

The book made an international impact and almost immediately she was drawn into the emerging Healing Movement. This twenty two year old young women was in demand as a speaker, sharing platforms with well known 'faith healers' of the day such as A.B. Simpson, A.J. Gordon and W.E. Boardman.

She was invited by fellow American, Boardman to be a speaker at a Holiness and Healing Conference in London in 1885 but was unable to attend. William and Mary Boardman had opened *Bethshan* healing home in London in 1880 which in its heyday attracted over six hundred to its meetings. He wrote to Carrie, 'Thousands know of you, as you are aware in this Kingdom [Britain], through your *Prayer of Faith* and lesser publications'. Twenty five years later she and her husband found this to be true as they met people whose lives had been impacted by her writings as they went on a world tour in 1909.

Triumphs Of Faith

Triumphs of Faith was a magazine which was widely read in Britain and to which the Boddys subscribed. She began its publication in 1881 and continued as its editor for sixty six years. It contained articles on the subjects of Holiness and Healing and after her Pentecost began to contain articles on the Baptism in the Holy Spirit and the world wide impact of this outpouring. It also chronicled the many ministries that were part of her life.

After her visit to Sunderland in 1909 Alexander commended the publication to the readers of *Confidence* explaining how to receive their copies. He also published several articles from *Triumphs* in *Confidence*. The power of the written word cannot be underestimated and through this avenue alone Carrie influenced a generation of readers.

Faith Rest Cottage

In 1882 Carrie established a faith healing home in Buffalo, New York where people could come and stay, receive teaching on faith and in an atmosphere of peaceful reflection receive prayer for the healing of body and soul. The roots of the 19th and 20th century Healing Movement lie in Europe as did the concept of a 'Healing Home' and *Faith Rest Cottage* was one of the first healing homes in the States. It became well known in the Healing Movement and even the secular press reported the cures that took place there.

Immediately following her healing she had began to pray for people in the room where she had been healed. Following this she began weekly meetings in her home. *Faith Rest Cottage* seemed a natural step from where Carrie was able to develop her ministry of prayer, teaching, writing and publishing...for a while at least!

Enter George

Little did Carrie know that her life was soon to change. She had decided to remain single until one day in 1889, in Chicago, she met a wealthy Californian business man called George Montgomery who had made his money in mining and property. The two were married within the year and she was whisked off to her new home in San Francisco.

For more than forty years the couple worked as a team. Only the Lord could have bought together the two entrepreneurs whose synergy enabled Carrie's ministries to flourish as they did. Carrie carried the vision from the Lord and George provided the funding to make it happen and supported her in every way.

Social Sickness

Carrie began to respond to the needs she saw in this frontier town. She not only continued to teach and pray for Divine Healing, holding regular parlour meetings in her home but ministered among the needy in the slums, prisons and saloons. She established, with George, the People's Mission of San Francisco and a girl's rescue home at Beulah, in nearby Oakland.

She had only been on the west coast three years when she opened The *Home of Peace* on land that George owned in Oakland across the Bay. It was to become a centre of ministry which continued to her death and is still used today by the Salvation Army.

Beulah Heights

The *Home of Peace* was a three storey Victorian mansion, a larger version of *Faith Rest Cottage,* which acted as a spiritual oasis where weary and sick in body, soul and spirit could find rest and be instructed in the ways of faith. It opened in 1893.

It was situated in an area called Beulah Heights which housed the Montgomery's multi-faceted ministries. Homes were built in the foothills for orphans and between 1894 and 1907 hundreds were cared for. It was a centre for missionaries on furlough and other mission related activities. Missionaries from one hundred societies used the home in one way or another. The Shalom Training School established in 1894 prepared men and women to be sent round the world.

The inhabitants of this 'town' needed a place to worship and the Montgomerys built Beulah Chapel. This was pastored by Carrie and later became part of the Assemblies of God.

A newspaper article in 1892 described the new town as a place 'where no dives were to be tolerated and around which…there would be a wall of morality so high that the devil couldn't climb over it'.

Round The World

Carrie always had an interest in mission. During the 1880s she became part of A.B. Simpson's Christian and Missionary Alliance and continued as a leader for over thirty years. It bought together different Holiness groups and taught Divine Healing. It also sent missionaries world wide.

So it was in 1909 that the newly Spirit Baptised Montgomerys made a round the world trip to see for themselves the Pentecostal outpourings in other lands. On the way back they called in at the 1909 Sunderland Convention before returning to Beulah Heights.

The Social Gathering

Every year at the Sunderland Convention there was a gathering of the guests in the Parish Hall where different nationalities present were introduced. Both Carrie and George were among those who gave their testimony to the Pentecostal blessing in June 1909. They told their respective stories and so shared with the others present and cemented the common bond of the Spirit Baptised.

They also bought greetings from the places they had been visiting. Carrie commented, 'It was worth going right round the world just to look in the face of one Chinese woman who was baptised in the Holy Ghost'. In India 'she met a dear native boy, so full of the Holy Ghost, that scintillations of light seemed to come from his face'.

They had also visited *Mukti Mission* near Poona (Pune), India and spoke of the marvellous scenes where hundreds of young widow girls had been baptised in the Holy Spirit at the home of Pandita Ramabai.

Known by reputation only, it was a coup for the young Pentecostal Movement in Britain to have this couple attending the four day convention. I'm sure that many women saw Carrie Judd Montgomery as a role model. She was a well respected woman with international influence and ministry experience in so many areas.

Many other men and women in the Holiness and Healing Movements had denounced 'speaking in other tongues' as demonic. That Carrie with her reputable cross denominational connections spoke in tongues and was one with them would have been such an encouragement.

No Fanaticism Or Excitement

On returning home to Beulah Heights she wrote an article about the Sunderland Convention for the readers of *Triumphs of Faith*. This was reprinted in the August 1909 edition of *Confidence*. One of her comments typified her preference for Pentecostal meetings, 'The meetings were quiet and powerful, with no fanaticism or excitement. Helpful Bible teaching was given by different pastors and teachers...'

Carrie was a woman who built bridges between different denominations and movements. Unity was a major theme of her ministry and so the unity she found at Sunderland was noteworthy. She wrote, '...we realized that though in some cases religious training had been different, yet we were all blessedly one in Christ, one bread, one body, all having been made to drink into the one Spirit'.

She also commented on Mary Boddy's ministry who greatly impressed her. 'Mrs. Boddy has been wonderfully taught of God and has a rare gift of expounding His Word. Her Bible talks upon Holiness and Divine Healing were very clear and powerful'.

Still The Healer

There is no doubt that Divine Healing was at the core of Carrie's ministry. In the last of her articles that appears in *Confidence* (May 1915) called *A Message to the Sick,* she writes,

'As I realise what precious years of service for the Lord have been mine because the word of healing was spoken to me by the Great Physician, when I was raised from my dying bed in answer to the prayer of faith, I feel that I must continually proclaim to others that Jesus Christ is still the Healer of His people. Wherever I go I find multitudes of God's children who are afflicted in body, most of them having suffered many things'.

She taught Divine Healing for many years before her Baptism in the Holy Spirit but she wrote in 1908, '...never have we personally known such a constant indwelling of the Healer as since we received our Pentecostal baptism'.

Christ's Quickening Life

Even before her visit to Sunderland, the British Pentecostals were familiar with her theology of Divine Health and Healing. In Carrie, Alexander had discovered a woman whose spiritual journey paralleled that of his wife Mary's. Prior to receiving the gift of tongues they both expressed the Baptism in the Holy Spirit as a sanctification experience. They had both experienced physical healing and more importantly had an identical theology. Mary had written many articles and pamphlets on the subject and her understanding of healing was a foundational teaching of the new movement.

Both ladies, following their Pentecosts, had a vision of the cross and of the finished work of Christ. So following the testimony of her Spirit Baptism in the November issue of *Confidence* it is not surprising we find Carrie's article, *Christ's Quickening Life for the Mortal Body* drawing on the same scriptures that Mary used in her teachings *(Galatians 2:20, Romans 8:10-11, 2 Corinthians 4:11).*

She wrote, 'In proportion as we by faith realize that we have died with Christ, we realize that we also live with him...The resurrection life of Christ actually quickens our mortal body'.

She continued, 'Only as we momentarily take the heavenly supply can we be free from weakness and sickness'. She calls this a 'precious secret of the Lord' and her wish is that all the readers will have this revealed to them by the Holy Spirit.

It's In The Atonement

In the opening editorial of *Triumphs of Faith* she states clearly that it is her belief that on the cross Christ atoned not just for our sins but our diseases. '...let me say that what is true of this precious spiritual healing is likewise true of physical healing by 'The Great Physician'. Christ bore our sickness as well as our sins, and if we may reckon ourselves free from the one, why not from the other'.

This was Alexander and Mary's belief and in the first year of the movement, 1908, Mary's tracts on Divine Health and Healing were available and editions of *Confidence* carried this teaching.

In Carrie's article *A Year with the Comforter* she notes the difference in her life since receiving the Baptism in the Holy Spirit. She wrote, 'For many years He has been my Healer, working miracles again and again in delivering me from sickness and pain. Now the Spirit who raised Christ from the dead so quickens my mortal body that I drink, continually. Deep draughts of a life which is altogether beyond anything in the natural'.

The Residue Of Oil

In two articles taken from *Triumphs* and published in *Confidence* in October and November 1912, Carrie sets out clearly her belief that the Baptism in the Holy Spirit accompanied by the sign of tongues is a third work of grace.

With reference to the leper in *Leviticus 14* who had received the sanctifying touch of the blood and the oil, she explains that 'he was now by that very process in a position to receive 'the rest of the oil', saved, sanctified and anointed, he does not consider the mistake of considering the work complete and therefore does not withdraw himself from the place of blessing'.

She explains, 'Many receive the touch of the blood that do not receive the anointing of the oil and many who receive the anointing do not realise there is anything further for them'. The Residue of Oil referred then to the Promise of the Father, the personal Holy Ghost residing in the human heart.

One of Mary Boddy's phrases that we read again and again in her teaching is 'the oil follows the blood'. Her understanding was the same as Carrie's.

The Way Of Faith

Faith was the key to appropriating the truths of Scripture. Faith was the key to her life and ministry. Her first book was called *The Prayer of Faith*. Her successful magazine *Triumphs of Faith*. Her only child who was born in 1891 was appropriately named, Faith.

The first of her lengthy articles that was published in *Confidence* bore the title *Steps of Faith*. She wrote, 'The moment you have faith, that moment something is accomplished'. Faith for Carrie was not just wishful thinking or even hope but something tangible that you hold on to until the answer comes, like Abraham who believed the Word of God and was 'fully persuaded that God had the power to do what He had promised' *(Romans 4:18-22)*. His way was always the way of faith.

No Theology

In 1914, Carrie made an interesting comment, 'When the dear Lord healed me, I was a little Episcopalian girl and I believed He chose me because I had no theology'. During her life she certainly made up for that and her theology of faith and Divine Health and Healing was to influence many.

Sharing The Blessing

After Carrie's Baptism in the Holy Spirit, her *Home of Peace* in Beulah Heights didn't just open its doors to those needing healing. She was keen to share the blessing that she had received and so began to teach about the full blessing of Pentecost. Guests who stayed in the thirty rooms had the opportunity of fellowship and sharing their experiences. Missionaries especially were welcome and offered hospitality as a gift if they could not afford to pay. From this base she continued her writing and speaking schedule as well as developing numerous other local Pentecostal works.

Homes Of Rest

By the turn of the century healing homes and rest homes in one shape or another were spreading far and wide. 'Homes of Rest' or 'Homes of Peace' on the Montgomery model began to appear as far away as India, some even called *Beulah*. We have already seen how Catherine Price and Margaret Cantel opened their homes as Homes of Rest in London and in the column *Pentecostal Items* in *Confidence* there were always homes advertised in various parts of the country, usually run by women. In early 1911 a Pentecostal home of rest called *Murrayfield* opened its doors in Sunderland in the bracing position opposite the North Pier. It was opened with the 'co-operation of Mr. and Mrs. Boddy' for those who wanted to attend services at All Saints' or to consult the Boddys about Divine Healing or the Baptism in the Holy Spirit. Visitors were going to Sunderland from far and wide to 'catch the flame or get the gift in them stirred up again'.

In March 1911 another home was opened called *Gillside*. It commanded a position overlooking the sea in Roker and had a private gate into Roker Park. There were 'beautiful turret rooms' with views across the sea and harbour and trams stopping at its door.

The weather would be a little more invigorating than its Stateside counterpart but the idea, although less grand was the same. I'm sure reading about Carrie's work at Beulah Heights was a strong influence behind these homes.

An Intensely Busy Life

On one of his seven visits to America Alexander Boddy was the guest of the Montgomerys at their *Home of Peace*. He describes the time spent with them in *Confidence* (December 1912) and illustrates the article with photos taken with his newly acquired Kodak Brownie. Alexander appreciated the peaceful surroundings and from his window he could see the villas and cottages scattered across the mountains.

He wrote, 'Mrs. Montgomery leads an intensely busy life. The telephone is often going and her secretary is often helping her'. He attended some of her meetings and was able to say, 'Mrs. Montgomery has the confidence of Christian people in this place'.

Sane, Able Teachers

Having secured a personal friendship with Carrie and George, Alexander was invited to be one of the speakers at a camp meeting that she was organising in Cazadero, California in July 1914. The land belonged to the Montgomerys and was aptly named *Elim Groves*. Amongst the giant redwood and cool streams it was an ideal place to seek the Lord. Accommodation was to be in tents but for the less adventurous a hotel, The Elim Hotel, was in the grounds.

At this time Carrie felt called of God to hold a World Wide Pentecostal Camp Meeting. She wrote, 'As His people come together in love and faith, we may trust Him for a great downpour of His Spirit; and that signs and wonders will be done in the name of His Holy Child, Jesus'.

Always wary of excess in Pentecostalism she commented 'We expect to have with us sane, able teachers and preachers who will 'rightly divide the Word of Truth,' under the anointing of the Holy Ghost'. She obviously thought Alexander fell into that category.

Alexander told the readers of *Confidence* about his invitation and said, 'The editor fully expects to have the privilege of being present'. Carrie expected the camp meeting to last at least a month or longer as the Lord led them.

Westward Ho!

So it was in June 1914 that Alexander set off for an extended trip to the States hoping to spend the last two weeks at Cazedero. Little did he know that his journey would be cut short when Germany invaded France and Russia at the end of July heralding the beginning of the First World War which for Britain began on August 4th.

The camp attracted eminent Pentecostal leaders of the day including Smith Wigglesworth. Alexander gave his impressions of the camp in an article he called, *Westward Ho!* in *Confidence* (Dec 1914). He was obviously mightily impressed with this woman and told his readers yet again that they would 'do well to subscribe to her monthly magazine'. He also used a photograph of Carrie as the 'cover girl' to this edition of *Confidence.*

He recalls that there were many healings and baptisms [in the Spirit]. He wrote,

> 'The scenes at the evening meetings were sometimes almost amazing. The people in this land are very responsive, and when a stirring address was ended they flung themselves on their knees round the platform...general prayer went up all over the gathering, there was strong crying often merging into praise. Then the Heavenly anthem til all arms went up and nearly every throat was thrilling with melodious notes, and then all were next on their feet raising higher the forest of uplifted arms, and the upturned faces radiant under the bright of the lamps'.

Even among such spiritual fervour he was able to say, 'Mrs. Carrie Judd Montgomery's name was a guarantee against fanaticism or wild fire, and the meetings were controlled by the Spirit'.

Farewells

Apart from an article in *Confidence* in May 1915, entitled *A Message to the Sick* this is the last time we read of Carrie in *Confidence*. It is fitting then that we record the farewells between Alexander and Carrie and George. He described the moment, 'I knelt with beloved Brother and Sister Montgomery in earnest prayer, and they committed me to the Lord for this long return journey with all its possibilities of danger from warships and mines'.

He returned safely to Sunderland after a two month's absence. Still remembered by Carrie, it is interesting that in 1927 she wrote to Alexander asking him to attend a conference in Lausanne but he was unable to do so. As Carrie Judd Montgomery continued her various ministries she was never to visit these shores again but her influence lived on in her writings and in the lives of the many she touched. She died in 1946 aged eighty eight years.

Faith Expressed Through Love

Carrie was an inspiring woman of faith and it was a faith rooted in reality. The Apostle Paul says, *'The only thing that counts is faith expressing itself through love' (Galatians 5:6)* and she was certainly a tender hearted woman of love and compassion.

The healing homes that she established were places where the sick were healed by the prayer of faith in an atmosphere of love. Weary missionaries found an oasis of peace in which to rest and seekers after the Baptism in the Holy Spirit were able to lay aside the cares of life and seek after God.

Her life is a reminder that no matter what we accomplish it is love that people will remember and all who knew her agreed that it was love which was the prominent feature in her life and work.

In an article in *Triumphs of Faith* written shortly after she was Baptised in the Holy Spirit she expressed a sentiment similar to that of Paul in *1 Corinthians 13*.

'We may have thought that we need other credentials, such as gifts of healing, miracles, gifts of tongues etc., while all these gifts of the Holy Ghost are most desirable and precious and useful, yet the main thing, the most mighty thing, which must be the foundation for every other equipment for service is the love of God shed abroad in our hearts by the Holy Ghost'.

Carrie Judd Montgomery was a significant role model for other women in the emerging Pentecostal Movement in Britain. Her godly character, experience in missions and evangelism, knowledge of Divine Healing and social concern coupled with her prolific and able writings, made her an example to follow.

Her life challenges us to allow the love of God to be our motivation and to express that love in a myriad of ways. In the lonely, sometimes friendless world in which we live, Homes of Rest and Homes of Peace are needed like never before. You never know, perhaps someone reading this chapter will be motivated by the love of God to do what Carrie did all those years ago and provide a place of healing and hope in a sad and broken world.

7

Leith Docks c1920

Christina Beruldsen
A Beautiful Work

'There is a beautiful work going on in Edinburgh.
Mrs. Beruldsen is deeply taught of God...
The household [is] all the Lords'

Miss Haggie

Following her Baptism in the Holy Spirit on January 4th 1908, Christina Beruldsen found herself being a busy lady. She commented, 'When we get lost in Him we do not need to look for work, the Lord sends plenty of work. It is no more trying, it's 'being led''. And the Lord certainly filled her hands. She pioneered and led Pentecostal meetings in her home which later developed into a regular Sunday gathering in the city of Edinburgh. In the same year, 1911, she opened a mission at Leith Docks, a rough area of the city.

The 'beautiful work' continued in the home where her five children were saved and filled with the Spirit, three of whom went to China as missionaries. As well as combining her wifely duties, motherhood, ministry and leadership she was a speaker at conventions around Britain and at the annual ones in Edinburgh which she hosted.

So it was indeed the truth when a Miss Haggie, after visiting the Edinburgh Convention of 1911, wrote in *Confidence*,

> 'There is a beautiful work going on in Edinburgh. Mrs. Beruldsen is deeply taught of God, showing in her life the gifts of the Spirit. The household all the Lords, from the head of the house, the dear husband, a true follower of the Lamb of Calvary, and out in the full salvation; and all the family of sons and daughters baptised in the Holy Spirit showing to the world, 'whom they are and whom they serve'. Hallelujah! Praise the Lord!'

The Norwegian Connection

Christina Cairns married Eilif[1] Beruldsen on July 12th 1879 in North Leith, Edinburgh, Scotland. Eilif had been a sea captain but following the wedding settled in Leith and became a prosperous ship chandler. He was Norwegian and never became a naturalised British subject. Both of their fathers had been in the merchant navy but Christina's father John had died while she was a child. Born in Leith in 1859, she was the middle child of a family of six and her mother, also Christina, had to work to look after the family by running a general shop. Christina was not allowed the luxury of staying on at school and by the age old twelve she was apprenticed to a dressmaker. Christina was twenty when she married and Eilif was two years her senior.

Between 1881 and 1890 the couple had five children, Einar, John, Christina, Thyra and Joseph. Eilif's job took him back and forth to Norway where three of their children were born. In the 1880s the family spent at least two extended periods in Norway, one possibly for three years. This would explain how Christiana was fluent enough in the language to act as an interpreter to the Norwegian party at the Sunderland Conventions.

Eilif's business prospered and his son, Einar joined the family firm and together they employed a number of people. Like many other middle class families they were able to have a live in servant and Swedish Elfreda became part of the Beruldsen household. It's interesting that most of our other 'forgotten women' had domestic help and were certainly not from the working classes except perhaps some of our missionary ladies. In the first part of the 20th century household duties were arduous and time consuming and the ladies we have featured were fortunate enough to have that burden taken from them.

A Growing Hunger

The Beruldsens attended Charlotte Baptist Chapel in Edinburgh where Eilif was an elder. In 1906 there had been a Holiness revival there which increased their hunger for more of God. Then they heard that in Norway many were beginning to be baptised in the Holy Spirit and speak in tongues. This was happening in a church in Oslo whose pastor, Thomas B. Barrett, carried the flame back home from a visit he made to the States in 1906. Barrett had been born in Cornwall, England and as a child accompanied his father, who was a mining engineer, to Norway. So the couple's interest grew, especially since this was happening in Eilif's native and Christina's adopted land by marriage. God was using a natural connection to awaken their interest and further His plans and purposes.

In August 1907, Alexander Boddy invited Barrett to his parish in Sunderland for a series of meetings. Within several weeks twenty five had received the Baptism with the sign of tongues. Initially Christina was sceptical of some of the manifestations but her husband was keen to invite Barrett to Edinburgh. Christina was actually quite relieved when she heard he had returned to Norway.

No Escape

But the Lord had plans for this woman. Christina couldn't escape! On January 1st and 2nd 1908, Alexander and Mary Boddy spoke at a Faith Mission Conference in Edinburgh. They told the story of the outpouring of the Holy Spirit since Pastor Barrett's visit to Sunderland.

Eilif and Christina were among those who attended. Christina's heart was touched and she now believed that the Lord had sent the Boddys to Edinburgh instead of Barrett. She said, 'I went to their meetings and there got such a longing to give myself wholly to God'.

Receiving 'The Blessing'

No encouragement was needed when two days after the conference, Eilif asked his wife if she would go to Sunderland. They didn't waste any time and by 7 o'clock that evening they had arrived. After finding somewhere to stay they went to the 9 o'clock Saturday night meeting in the vestry at All Saints'. Christina described what happened in *Confidence* (April 1908).

> 'I shall never forget the solemnity of that meeting and the holy awe in that place. No one lifted their head or looked up when we went in. They seemed to be wholly taken up with God. After they had sung a chorus Mrs. Boddy said, 'Shall we have a season of prayer'.
>
> I got up and asked them to pray for us as we had come from Edinburgh to get the blessing. We all knelt down and how they prayed; they seemed to know how to lay hold of God. In a very short time I felt the power of God coming upon me; my whole being seemed to be filled with a calm rest and peace. Then Mrs. Boddy came over and said, 'I feel led by the Spirit to lay hands on your head'. I said, 'Praise God, I'm going to get the blessing now''.

After answering some questions about her relationship with the Lord and whether there was any unforgiveness in her heart, Mary Boddy said, 'Receive ye the Holy Ghost' and 'By simple faith,' she said, 'I received the Holy Ghost'.

Speaking In Tongues

At that time Christina didn't speak in tongues but she continues the story in this way.

> 'On Wednesday the eighth, the Lord seemed to say to me, 'Would you not like the rest of the blessing?' I really felt as if I had got so much that I hardly knew how I could contain

more, but I just said, 'Lord, I will take all Thou hast for me' and yielded myself entirely to Him. That evening the meeting was in the dining room of the vicarage. After the meeting had gone on for about two hours I felt a peculiar struggle going in my throat'.

Then after some prayer her 'tongue was loosed' and she spoke in tongues for two hours. She recalls,

'All through the night I was singing heavenly music. I cannot express in words the sweet communion and adoration that filled my whole being. The next forenoon I again spoke for two hours'.

Eager to understand what she had been saying she asked God to give her the interpretation which was, 'You shall preach Jesus to poor sinners'. She then felt the Lord speak to her about the country, Peru. Ten days later back home at the mission hall a young man heard her testimony and when she mentioned Peru he felt assured this was the country God was calling him to.

Eilif's Blessing

It would seem that Eilif received his 'blessing' at the church service on the Sunday where he experienced the wonderful presence and power of the Holy Ghost. He recommitted his life to the Lord telling Him he would follow Him fully and would put everything right in his life as the Lord showed what to do. From that moment, as he testified in 1917, 'God had been with him and blessed him graciously'.

Healed

At the same time she received the Holy Spirit, Christina was healed of an unknown physical condition. She couldn't eat any solid food and had seen the doctor daily for six months. Apparently he was amazed when she went back home. So many other of our 'forgotten women' had experienced divine healing and in each case it deepened their relationship with God as Mary, Lydia, Carrie, Eleanor, Polly and Mabel, one of the secretaries, all testified.

In 1912 Christina gave her testimony.

> 'When I came to Sunderland first I was on the edge of the
> grave - a thin, delicate thing. Am I that today? When the
> Lord baptised me in the Holy Ghost and fire He burned up
> all the disease in my body. I bought all my medicine [t]here
> with me, but I never touched it'.

A New Mother

On Sunday, the very day after receiving her Baptism she wrote home
to her family and told them they had got a new mother - body, soul and
spirit. Her physical body had been healed, her frayed emotions had
been stilled and her spirit quickened by the power of the Holy Ghost.

In her own words, 'I have been a Christian for many years but have
lived an up and down life, sometimes bright but oftener depressed
and downcast'. She had been searching and now she had discovered
peace. For six years she had attended consecration and Holiness
meetings and even been baptised in water to try and obtain what she
felt was lacking in her life.

But now she could say, 'My life is changed completely. I am
praising my Saviour day and night...Once I sought the blessing, but
now it's 'Himself'. Oh the joy of knowing Jesus, no more worry just
a calm rest, abiding in Him...my daily experience is that to 'trust and
obey' is the secret of a happy life'.

Bringing Forth Fruit

As she went home to Edinburgh she prayed this prayer, 'That I may be
kept very humble and also that I may be a living branch in the vine, that
I may bring forth much fruit to His glory'. And the Lord answered.

As soon as she arrived back home she started 'waiting meetings' in
her beautiful house, *Solberg*, in Murrayfield Gardens, Edinburgh on
Tuesday afternoons and evenings. Those who were hungry to receive
the Baptism of the Holy Spirit were invited to come and be prayed
for. It was a feature of this revival that the blessing was transferable
and especially those who had travelled to Sunderland caught the fire
and took the flame back home with them and passed it on.

By August 1908 we read in *Confidence* that she was working with a Mrs. McPherson who also held meetings in her home twice a week after experiencing a miraculous healing. Christina comments, 'Last week a lady 'came through' ([she writes] I do not like that expression) speaking in a clear beautiful language, then sang three verses of a hymn in an unknown tongue'. Another wrote, 'In Mrs. Beruldsen's home…God came among us so blessedly, we were nearly three hours in the meeting and didn't realise it'.

These meetings were just the beginning.

Sunderland Again

In the very first issue of *Confidence* (April 1908) there is a letter from Mrs. C. Beruldsen. In it she wrote her testimony to Mr. and Mrs. Boddy saying it was her duty to do so in order that it may help someone.

Then in June of the same year she and her husband and daughter travelled by a train especially hired for the occasion to take Scottish Pentecostal people to the first Sunderland Convention. Her co-worker Mrs. McPherson was with them.

There they joined a party from Scandinavia which included Laura, Pastor Barrett's wife and two Norwegian sisters, Dagmar Gregersen and Agnes Thelle who had a prophetic ministry. Although Eilif was there with them it was Christina who did all the interpreting.

The First Edinburgh Conference

Encouraged and envisioned by the Sunderland Conference, Christina and Mrs. McPherson organised their first conference in Edinburgh for October 17th and 18th of the same year. Friends came from all over Scotland, forty from one town alone. The main speaker was Mary Boddy who spoke on the coming of the Lord.

A report of the conference in *Confidence* says,

> 'The meetings were characterised by a restful calm and quick excitement or fleshly emotion were conspicuous by their absence, while at the concluding gathering on Sunday night God set His seal of blessing by a wave of power which suddenly broke over the entire audience'.

One feature noted was the 'complete absence of anything like human leadership or control'. Yet there was perfect order as the Holy Spirit was allowed to have His way.

These two sisters were so encouraged by the seal of God's approval on the gatherings that they planned to arrange another conference for the next month. There is no evidence as to whether this took place but we do know that the two ladies were speakers at a conference in Carlisle at the end of November.

The Conferences Continue

However, from January 1910 conferences in Edinburgh continued annually and were still happening in 1917. The prominent Pentecostal leaders of the time were often the speakers. At the first conference there had been Alexander Boddy and Cecil Polhill. Later ones included the ministry of Mary Boddy, Pastor Niblock from the PMU, Pastor T.M. Jeffreys from Wales and Eleanor Crisp of the Ladies' Training Home.

Alexander wrote in *Confidence*, 'It was good to meet Mrs. Beruldsen and her family...A little room behind the platform was used as a power station and amid earnest prayer and sometimes a rush of tongues as the Spirit gave utterance, seekers were welcoming blessing for themselves and others'.

Mary Boddy was the main speaker the next year. Christina met the party from Sunderland at the station and whirled Mary off in a taxi to Murrayfield Gardens. After a rest they all joined together at her home where there was a time of praise and prayer until 10 o'clock.

These conferences were held at the Protestant Institute, Edinburgh and at the first meeting we are told, 'The hall [was] well filled with earnest, eager men and women [who] met together to hear of Jesus and His work; [and] seekers and hungry hearted Christians longing for more of Himself'.

During the afternoons Christina opened her home to seekers of Baptism of the Holy Spirit where they were 'dealt with... with God greatly blessing and bringing into liberty and joy many dear souls'.

The London Declaration

It is a credit to her standing among the Pentecostal leaders in Britain that in November 1910, Christina was one of the thirty signatories of a statement of belief called 'The London Declaration'. It was entitled 'The Baptism in the Holy Ghost – What we teach concerning the evidence and the results'. This was the answer to the anti-Pentecostal 'Declaration of Berlin' delivered to the German leaders in September by pastors who opposed the Pentecostal experience of tongues.

Mrs. McPherson's signature also appears but Eilif Beruldsen's didn't, which is an indication that although in full sympathy with his wife, it was she who took the public role. We always read of the meetings in Edinburgh being led by Mrs. Beruldsen and this is born out by two comments, both written by Alexander in *Confidence*. In 1917 he wrote, 'Since their first visit to Sunderland in 1907… Mrs. Beruldsen has led the good work which is now conducted in their Leith Mission'. In 1916, 'Mrs. Crisp addressed the assembly established by Mrs. Beruldsen'. Later Pentecostal historians seemed to have struggled with the idea of female leadership saying the work was led by her husband, but I suppose they were men of their time who found this in conflict with their theology.

'Sabbath' Meetings Start

The Lord continued to bless the work in Edinburgh even though she acknowledged it was a difficult place in which to minister. But the work had become established enough by March 1911 for Christina to begin Sunday meetings. Regular 'Sabbath' meetings at 11am were announced in *Confidence*, to be held at the Protestant Institute, Bridge, Edinburgh, the same place as the conferences were held. She was able to say that they were experiencing the power of God with a steady stream of sinners saved, sanctified and filled with the Holy Spirit.

A 'Soul Saving Work'

During the same year Christina and her helpers begun a mission at Leith Docks. Edinburgh is a sea port and like many other ports at that time the area around the docks was often run down and the home of the poorer stratum of society. Drunkeness would have been rife. It is here that her husband carried out his business and Christina would have been familiar with the social challenges of such a place.

Fuelled by a passion for the lost, this middle class woman held open air meetings at the docks and many drunkards were 'reclaimed'. Alexander called it a 'soul saving work'.

A report in *Confidence* (August 1910) tells of 'remarkable times of blessings in the Mission Hall in Leith'. It continues, 'Many have been baptised in the Spirit, or healed of sicknesses. A Russian young lady recently was baptized in the Spirit…she saw happiness on the faces of the Pentecostal people that she had never seen in Christians before. This attracted her to the Lord'.

Victory Over Drink

It must be remembered that this period in history was noted for its Temperance Societies so the story written in *Confidence* in 1912 in a fuller form than space permits here would have met with great approval. It was entitled, *Victory Over Drink*.

Alexander wrote that it was, 'A story sweetly told by Mrs. Beruldsen at Sunderland…in whose mission at Leith the incident took place'.

In this case the drunkard was a wife and mother. Her desperate husband went down to 'the lady at the mission' for advice. There was a prayer meeting going on and she told him he needed to get his soul saved. They got him to his knees and soon he was saved. On returning home his wife said, 'Why John you've got something you hadn't when you went out. What is it?'

'Oh Mary, I forgi'e ye everything. I got converted', her husband replied.

'The Lord took all the desire for drink from her and now she and her husband and children are witnesses and workers for Jesus in that mission'. What a happy ending and such a change from the stories where it was the husband who had the drink problem!

Such was their commitment to this work that in March 1914 the Beruldsens moved house to be nearer the mission in Leith. Their new address was in Laverock Bank Terrace in Trinity, a suburb of Edinburgh.

Pentecost In The Home

In their home practical results followed the blessings of Pentecost. Like every Christian mother, her heart's desire was for her five children to come to know the Saviour whom she loved so dearly.

She was able to stand up at a Pentecostal conference in Edinburgh in 1910 and say she had all five grown up children sitting in the meeting, filled with the Holy Ghost.

Let her give her testimony as she told it at the 1910 Sunderland Conference,

> 'I do plead with the mothers. I believe they do have such an influence in the home. I prayed for my children twenty six years but the Lord did it all in thirteen months. Hand yourself over to the Holy Ghost. He will do everything. When He baptised me He said, 'The promise is for you and your children's children and to all that are afar off'.
>
> I said, 'Lord, are they all going to get what I have got?' and from that moment I stopped praying for my children, and I began to praise the Lord because He had given me the assurance, and within thirteen months they were all rejoicing in the Baptism of the Holy Ghost. Hallelujah!'

Many visitors to their home commented how they were inspired by the whole household's devotion to the Lord. They were indeed a witness to the world!

Missionaries Of Us All

'The Baptism of the Holy Ghost makes missionaries of us all; it sends us out to the lost. It sent three of our family to China and those left at home out into the open air preaching the Gospel'. So said Christina at the 1912 Sunderland Conference.

Her children that went to China were John (26), Christina (24) and Thyra Beruldsen (22). They were some of the earliest missionaries sent out by the PMU. John was to serve in North China for thirty five years. Both girls married in the field, Christina to Mr. Parley Guldbrandsen and Thyra to Mr. Percy Bristow.

Confidence reports in August 1910,

'Mr. and Mrs. Beruldsen of 'Solberg', Murrayfield Gardens, Edinburgh, are willingly giving up their first born son and their two much loved daughters for China's needs. After training in the London homes of our PMU they go forth now as three of our missionaries. A God sent opening, we believe, has presented itself in the Tsili or (Chi-li) Mission in North China, to which they have been invited, and with the cordial approval of the PMU they go out to work at Suen-hwa-fu, near Pekin [Beijing]. They go by steamer this month (August)'.

They actually left on 13th September departing from Waterloo Station in London to embark on the *Princess Alice* at Southampton. A letter written by John from the port of Algiers describes their send off at Waterloo. Imagine the scene!

'There were some fifty of our Pentecostal friends [including Eilif and Christina] seeing us off and we joined in singing, 'Far, far away in heathen darkness dwelling', 'No never alone' and 'God be with you til we meet again''.

An open air meeting on the platform, but then Christina was used to that back at the docks.

It Reminds Me Of A Time

Her children's letters home appeared regularly in *Confidence* and make interesting reading, telling of the hardships and the victories of these early missionary pioneers. Their compassion for the Chinese and their longing to see them come to Christ is evident from their writing.

In 1914, John wrote in a letter to his mother. 'We are having prayer meetings every night. We have them in our own sitting room. The meetings we have had have lasted about three hours and then the people don't want to go away. It reminds me of the time we had five years ago'.

The children carried with them to China the example that their mother had lived out before them at Murrayfield.

We glean another insight about the Beruldsen home from a comment made by a Mr. Swift after he stayed with them in 1915.

'Missionaries have their pictures in a prominent place over the fireplace, and one occasionally hears someone pray for 'the mantelpiece', meaning friends in the regions beyond'.

Perfect Peace

What was it like for a mother to send three children from this close knit family to China? Would she ever see them again? The political situation was unstable and there was the distinct possibility they would die of some tropical disease on a foreign field. Missionaries had to be willing to lose their lives for the sake of the Gospel unless they were all caught up to meet the Lord in the air *(1 Thessalonians 4:17)*.

At the 1910 Sunderland Convention Christina had pleaded with Pentecostal parents to give their children to the Lord's work. She trusted God to look after them and give her peace.

Two years later at the 1911 Sunderland Convention she relates a vision she had had the previous year which bought her comfort.

'I saw my Saviour and He looked at me with such pitying eyes. He had a crimson mantle on. He did not say a word, but He opened His mantle and laid me right in, and I know now what it means. The Lord has kept me in perfect peace this year'.

She continued,

'Many of you know what has been going on in China[2] but it has never touched us. Hallelujah. That is what the Baptism in the Holy Ghost can do - keep one in perfect peace. I have met people and they have been almost afraid to speak, but I was rejoicing in the Lord through it all because He loves them'.

Later Years

We read in 1917 that Eilif had been 'absolutely at death's door' but 'was raised by prayers and faith of those around him'. At the 1917 Edinburgh Conference he testified and looked 'brighter than ever'. The works in Edinburgh and Leith were still going strong and their home was still being used for smaller gatherings.

In 1920, the then young Donald Gee, who was later to become a leading figure in the Pentecostal Movement in Britain, took over their assembly. In 1922, Eilif gave him a small piece of land at Bonnington Toll to erect a new wooden building for a church.

In 1923 the Beruldsens emigrated to Australia. Eilif had retired, Christina was sixty four and the opportunity arose for them to spend the remaining years of their life taking it easier on the other side of the world.

This godly family, and Christina Beruldsen especially, had certainly made their mark in the early years of the Pentecostal Movement in Britain.

No Limits!

A century ago we read of a woman of God who rose to the challenge of leadership and at the same time conducted her affairs in the home in such a way to bring glory to the Lord.

As she was led by the Spirit she embraced the callings that He placed upon her, taking a public ministry role. In the early years of Pentecostalism this was accepted as a result of the Holy Spirit being outpoured on the sons and the daughters in equal measure.

One can draw a certain parallel with Phoebe *(Romans 16:1-2)* who was a *diakonos* (Gk) in the church in Cenchrea. In all other cases in the New Testament this is translated as 'minister' rather than 'servant' as it is here and indicates that she held a position of authority in the church. Paul doesn't just call Phoebe a *diakonos* but a *prostatis* which shows her role was that of an overseer. She was certainly trusted by the Apostle Paul to take a letter to the Roman Church which was four hundred miles away from Corinth and had been a great help to many people including Paul himself. Some first century woman!

Cenchrea was a Greco-Roman sea port six miles east of Corinth. Such was the reputation of Old Corinth that Aristophanes (450-385 BC) coined the verb to *corinthianize* which meant to *fornicate*. Cenchrea, like the sea port of Edinburgh would have been a challenging place to minister, especially for a woman.

But it's women like Christina who were pioneers in regard to ministry and leadership. It would seem that we have lost ground to make up in this regard. She was not just involved in ministry but is what we would call today a 'church planter', first in her home and then 'going public' in the city. She was a speaker at national conferences and a signatory of a national declaration. A 20th century *diakonos* and *prostatis*.

Women of God, be encouraged! A century ago women didn't even have the vote, yet among the community of Pentecostal Spirit Baptised Christians there were no limits at least in the early days. Take the lid off, there are no restrictions placed upon you only those of your own making. Is there a 'beautiful work' that God is calling you to do?

---

1 This is the spelling used by Donald Gee in *Wind and Flame* but *Ellef* is the spelling on the marriage certificate

2 See Chapter 11, *Missionary Ladies*

8

The Secretaties They Worked Hard!

*'Two faithful Secretaries are daily at work,
and at times very hard at work'*

Alexander Boddy

Behind every revival there is a lot of hard work. As waves of the Spirit roll over meetings and people thrill as the presence of God invades their lives, behind the scenes servant hearted men and women just plain work hard using their varying gifts to enable others to be blessed. Margaret E. Howell and Mabel C. Scott were two such women. They were known as Miss Howell and Miss Scott, 'The Secretaries', who had been led by the Holy Spirit to go to live in Sunderland in August 1907.

God had a work for them to do the scope of which they would never have imagined when they arrived just prior to the outpouring of the Spirit at the beginning of September. They were responsible for sending out all the literature from Sunderland which informed the world of the revival. They dispatched countless issues of *Confidence*, helped organise the Sunderland Conventions, wrote letters and responded to requests for booklets and tracts. This they did faithfully until July 1910.

She Will Be Given More

God honoured their faithfulness and entrusted them with more. Whilst continuing their administrative duties they started a successful evangelistic work among the poor people in Fulwell Road, the same road as All Saints' Church. They also took girls into their home and trained them for domestic service or what ever else the Lord had for them.

We glean a picture of two hard working women of faith and integrity who responded to the call of God. It's partly because of them we know so much about the early days of the Pentecostal Movement. Without their diligence the other chapters of this book may have not been written.

The Secretaries' Testimony

It was a prominent feature of the early days that everyone tell the testimony of how they were baptised in the Holy Spirit with the sign of tongues or how the Lord had healed them. So it's no surprise to see in the very first issue of *Confidence* in April 1908, *Our Secretaries' Testimony*. It seems that they experienced their Spirit Baptism together at the same time on the first day of Pastor Barratt's special meetings that heralded the beginning of the revival. So they were two of the very first of the twenty five people who were to receive in Sunderland over the next six weeks. They wrote,

> 'God gave us this confidence and directed us to come
> to Sunderland and wait here with his children for our
> 'Pentecost' with signs following. He heard us and on the

night of Sunday, September 1ˢᵗ 1907, He came suddenly; as He had promised, and filled these temples with His glory, simultaneous speaking through us with new tongues, filling us to the overflow with the joy of His presence'.

I wonder if it was their suggestion the magazine should be named *Confidence*? The confidence they had was in the sure knowledge that God would hear them when they prayed according to His will *(1 John 5:14)*. They believed that the Holy Spirit would only fill a 'cleansed temple' and that first they needed the witness through the Word of God of a clean heart in line with the Holiness teaching of the day.

They wrote this testimony seven months after they had received and both agreed, 'It is all of God, the work is His, and the fire will spread until all the world shall know the salvation of God'. Mabel Scott also testified at the Sunderland Convention in June of that year that God had given her a new life because she had been healed of rheumatism.

Daily At Work

These ladies were at the epicentre of what God was doing in Britain and the shock waves reached the ends of the earth. Sunderland was a centre of blessing and many visited taking the fire back home with them. Testimonies and letters poured in telling what was happening in different parts of the world. The Secretaries answered them. Sunderland was also a centre which sent out free literature explaining different theological truths which underpinned the revival and testimonies of blessing. The Secretaries sent it out.

Alexander Boddy must have been so grateful that the Lord had provided these two dear sisters who gave their time and talents voluntarily. He commented in *Confidence*,

'Scores of thousands of testimonies and other publications have been sent for, and have travelled to Jamaica, Cuba, Canada, USA, India, South Africa, Switzerland, Holland, Italy, Ireland, Wales, Scotland and all parts of England. Two faithful Secretaries are daily at work, and at times very hard at work, letter writing and despatching literature'.

A Silent Missionary

Then in April 1908, seven months after the beginning of the revival the Lord put it in the heart of vicar, Alexander, to edit and publish *Confidence*, 'A Free Pentecostal Paper'. It was the first British paper that told of this outpouring with the sign of tongues. The importance of the magazine cannot be overestimated in spreading the message. He wrote,

> 'It is meant to be a means of grace and mutual encouragement. Encouragement to lonely ones and scattered bands, to those who are attacked by doubt and difficulty, but longing to be loyal to the Almighty Deliverer. They will find from these columns that they are not alone, as regards even human fellowship, but there are many that have perfect 'confidence' that this work is of God, and who will be rejoiced to know that His Pentecostal Blessing is spreading all the time'.

Why *Confidence*? On the cover there were two scriptures, *'This is the confidence we have in Him, that if we ask anything according to His will, He heareth us' (1 John 5:14 KJV)* and *'The Lord shall be thy confidence and shall keep thy foot from being taken' (Proverbs 3:16 KJV)*. The title pointed to confidence in the faithfulness of God to answer prayer and give the Holy Spirit to those who simply asked as in the case of Margaret and Mabel.

And it was free because Alexander wanted it to be 'a far reaching silent missionary of God's truth'. He hoped it would continue until Jesus came which he believed was an event not to far away.

Between April 1908 and 1926 there were one hundred and forty one issues and for the first two to three years The Secretaries were responsible for dispatching them and handling all the associated mail. By January 1910 around four thousand were sent out monthly and with an average of five readers a copy, it was estimated there were twenty thousand readers altogether. According to Alexander this involved the handling of three tons of paper over three years.

World Wide Circulation

Alexander boasted that the paper travelled to nearly every country on the globe where English was understood. Grateful letters assured him the message was getting through and was being a blessing. As editor he decided what it contained and so was able to put his stamp on the foundational theology of the movement.

He states what this is at the beginning of issues from 1910 having had a few years to evaluate this move of God.

> '*Confidence* advocates an unlimited Salvation for Spirit, Soul and Body; the Honouring of the Precious Blood; Identification with Christ in Death and Resurrection, etc; Regeneration, Sanctification; the Baptism of the Holy Ghost; the Soon-Coming of the Lord in the air *(1 Thessalonians 4:14)*; Divine Healing and Health *(Acts 4:13)*'.

Confidence also contained reports of the Sunderland and other conventions both home and abroad, testimonies and letters, a myriad of teachings and messages, a column, *Pentecostal Items* keeping readers up to date with other centres and extensive coverage of the missionary endeavour. From 1909 it acted as the authoritative voice of the Pentecostal Movement.

A Rare Anointing

Donald Gee in his history of the Pentecostal Movement, *Wind and Flame*, says that 'God honoured *Confidence* in a special way and was pleased to make it one of his principal channels to bring many in touch with the Pentecostal blessing'. It was 'highly treasured by hungry hearts'. He makes a pertinent comment that 'a rare anointing rested on those early issues'.

The life and movings of the Spirit of God were contained in its pages. Alexander commented in 1910 that '*Confidence*, like Pentecostal life, seems to be growing better all the time. This is not remarkable when the Lord gives such a splendid, Spirit filled staff

and special correspondents. It is His work and His paper'. The hard
work of Margaret Howell and Mabel Scott made all this possible and
the work was surrounded with prayer.

The Lord's Blessing On Each Copy

One would be forgiven for thinking that these two Edwardian spinsters
toiled on alone but a completely different picture emerges of their life.
They wrote about the days in their house when *Confidence* was about
to be dispatched. Instead of stoicism we are given a picture of fun.

> 'Imagine yourselves then at 11 Park Lea Road, Roker,
> towards the middle of the month, and you will hear instead
> of the quiet, which you may think reigns in the home of two
> steady-going secretaries, a chattering of young voices and
> the bustle of a busy household'.

Within a year of coming to Sunderland their house was full of needy
children who all helped in the work. Although they had three older
helpers to do the more complicated work the young girls considered
it a privilege to help put the copies in the envelopes, tie up the parcels
and stick on the stamps. Even the little baby they looked after was
entertained by watching them! And so a secret of *Confidence*'s
blessing? They explain,

> 'All the household prays over *Confidence* before it arrives,
> when it comes and when it sets forth on its travels…It takes
> three days to get all the copies packed up, and then the post
> cart calls and we all help carry it out and pray for the Lord's
> blessing on each copy and all who shall in any way help it
> on its way'.

I can just imagine the conversations where these two ladies talked
about the different places they are sending them too and keeping the
children enthralled with 'missionary stories' of boys and girls in far
away lands. One of the little helpers said how lovely it would be to
go on all the long journeys with the various parcels.

Women Of Integrity

The Secretaries were meticulous in their work. At the beginning of every issue every donation received was acknowledged and given a number. Then underneath a balance sheet of receipts and expenditure was printed. No doubt their ledgers were in good accounting order. They emerge as women of integrity who Alexander could trust with this important work. When in July 1910 the work passed on to Mr. and Mrs.William Busfield *Confidence* continued to flourish with the same circulation.

A Sad Story

One can't help but contrast this with the American counterpart to *Confidence*, called the *Apostolic Faith*, which was sent out from the Azusa Street Mission from 1906-8. Distributed free of charge it reached forty thousand readers across the world with five thousand copies sent out monthly. This was overseen by Clara Lum. who acted as secretary and co-editor and had built up a mailing list of twenty thousand.

The ending of the magazine *Apostolic Faith* as sent out from Azusa and describing the move of God from that place is a sad story.[1] In June 1908, Clara left to live and work in Oregon in another ministry taking the mailing list with her and refused to give Seymour any of the names. William Seymour was the leader of the revival in Azusa and this was a severe blow to the ministry there. It is thought she once hoped to be Seymour's wife but left the mission after he married Jennie Moore. I somehow can't imagine the two spinsters of the parish of All Saints' following her example.

Red And White Rosettes

Another duty these ladies handled was the administration behind the annual Whitsuntide Sunderland Conventions. They responded to requests for tickets and dealt with all correspondence concerning board and lodging. At the 1909 convention they would be instantly recognizable because they were wearing red and while rosettes. As the work grew they also handled all Alexander's correspondence.

Honour Where Honour's Due

They were introduced at the first Sunderland Convention. Behind the scenes workers deserve honour. It is heartening to see the value that Alexander placed on these women. We read of him calling them 'our much valued secretaries' on several occasions.

Each convention had what was called 'A Social Gathering', an informal meeting in the Parish Hall with afternoon tea, introductions, singing, testimonies and a short address.

The social gathering of June 1907 is described in this way, 'It was a truly happy family that thus met. The joyful faces, the words of kindly greeting, the bright singing from time to time and the testimonies of God's goodness made us feel it was a glimpse of heaven on earth'.

It was in this jovial atmosphere that Miss Howell and Miss Scot were invited on the platform to tell how they had come to be at Sunderland and how the Lord had blessed them with their Pentecost with the sign of tongues.

Gospel Teas

Their encounter with the Lord came with a call to work among the poor in Fulwell Road where the church was. All Saints' was a working class parish with all the inherent social problems that were part of life at the beginning of the 20th century.

In the early days of Pentecostalism the emphasis was on foreign missions and little is recorded of community work unless it is in direct relation to evangelistic missions. The Secretaries called their cottage meetings 'mission work'. It had a definite evangelistic thrust and also prepared those who were 'saved' to receive the Baptism in the Holy Spirit. Lives were changed and as a direct result social and material needs were met.

On two afternoons and three evenings a week those attending the gatherings could be seen tucking into buns served with tea and coffee provided by the members of All Saints'. These were called 'Gospel Teas'.

Mary and Alexander Boddy called this a 'remarkable evangelistic work' and saw it as an answer to years of prayer and supported them in every way. They were assisted by other Spirit Baptised members of the church.

A Remarkable Evangelistic Work

It started with the two Secretaries meeting the poor children in the church yard for a Bible talk and hymns. Apparently they met outside because it only happened if the weather permitted. Towards the end of 1908 they rented a room opposite the church. From the beginning the Lord set His seal on the work and soon the room couldn't hold all who came.

By February 1909 there were regular meetings for very poor children, women's meetings, a rope factory girls' meeting and men's meetings. More general meetings were held on Tuesday, Thursday, Saturday and Sunday evenings.

The two describe the blessings, 'Lips are opened as the Spirit of God descends on them in their meetings, a stream of prayer and praise and song ascends - sometimes right at the outset of the meetings'.

Over sixty had been saved, many had an assurance of a clean heart and several were baptised in the Holy Spirit and spoke in tongues. Only a few didn't return after their conversion, most came back again and again bringing the unsaved in.

We read of many wanting to get confirmed (a reminder that this was all going on in a parish of the Church of England). Others were encouraged to 'seek their Pentecost' on Sunday and Monday nights in the vestry. They commented that these people 'go as they are' and that this is a sign of their 'real heart hunger'. They were too poor to have any 'respectable clothes' associated with entering in a church, an interesting comment on the times.

The Vicar's Sunday afternoon Men's Bible Class was ever popular with these new converts. The Lord had especially worked among the men, and those who had been Spirit Baptised before were now being used to win 'rough men' for Christ.

This Is The Lord's Doing

Women testified to changed homes as the light of the Gospel entered family life. Most of the men were out of work due to depression in the ship building trade. But the testimony was always the same, 'Since they let Jesus into their hearts their needs have been supplied'. This was not through the mission but in other ways. It helped that a consequence of the Gospel was that men cleaned up their lives and gave up drink and tobacco which they could ill afford. One seven year old boy who had been barefoot all winter told the two ladies that he had prayed for boots on Monday and they came on Tuesday!

In writing the account for *Confidence* they say, *'This is the Lord's doing and it is marvellous in our eyes...we praise and give him all the glory. One soweth and another reapeth' (John 4:38 KJV).*

A Proof Of Pentecost

Following the report of their work in *Confidence* in February 1908, Alexander acknowledged how thankful he was for this work going on under the shadow of his church. He said it was 'one of the proofs of the blessed power given through the Baptism of the Holy Ghost with the sign of tongues'. He noted that those who were helping in the cottage mission were growing rapidly in spiritual power and experience. He believed that by soul winning, perhaps more than in any other way, the gifts were stirred up within us.

He also mentioned that as well as all the other things these ladies were doing they were 'also training young maidens for service and [were] depending entirely on the Lord'.

Feed My Lambs

Even though the work distributing *Confidence* reached to the ends of the earth, they didn't neglect their Jerusalem. As if they weren't busy enough they had, in obedience to God's call, taken poor girls into their home to train them for domestic service. This was considered a better option than factory work and trained girls would have the prospect of working in a good family.

The Lord gave them the command to 'feed His lambs'. He then showed them two girls of fourteen and fifteen to train and then a younger one of twelve. Then they took in two little ones who were in great need, aged five and fifteen months. All of these children had lost one parent. They had obeyed the call and were able to say, 'Now the little home of the Lord is full'.

A True Work

In November 1909, a year after they began to take in children Margaret and Mabel moved to a bigger house so they could expand their work. The new house was still in Roker and stood in its own grounds facing the sea. It was called *Peareth*.

Although they must have been ladies of some independent means they still needed to trust God for the work they were doing. We read of the 'marvellous way God had gone before, opening apparently brazen gates and making crooked places straight'. From time to time they offered hospitality to visitors but their main work was among needy children. For the time being they continued to act as secretaries. Five months later there were ten or twelve children living at the house who were supported by the generosity of God's people. One PMU student who had been there many times wrote,

> 'I am sure that it is a true work being carried on. They have taken in as the Lord directed, many from destitution and ill health, when the Lord has undertaken for them and has provided wonderfully...The care of these little ones entails much prayerful responsibility, for they are being taught their lessons and other things by these two servants of God. Oftentimes they have been put into sore straits in regard to food, but God has provided'.

He called for the 'prayers of all God's saints that God will supply, guide and overlook in all the many details connected with this house'.

Multiplying Potatoes

Feeding hungry children was expensive and on occasions funds were in short supply. It was then that the Lord performed miracles. Mabel relates one incident at a time of great testing at the home.

> 'On a Monday there were not enough potatoes in the cellar for the next day's dinner, We prayed as we do about everything and asked the Lord to supply the need, which He did not by sending more but by making those last to the following Thursday week. Day by day as we went down for potatoes there were sufficient for the day's need. Praise God! The days of His miracle working are not past. In many ways too numerous to mention has the Lord increased the food provided. When serving out what seemed a short supply there has always been enough and some to spare'.

Times like these served to strengthen their faith in their heavenly Father's goodness to them.

A Pentecostal House Warming

A month after moving into *Peareth* there was the official housewarming. It was on the shortest day of the year just before Christmas and the house was bright with the light of coal fires shining through the windows.

An afternoon tea meeting was held in the spacious entrance hall. The children were scrubbed and wearing their best clean dresses. It was a happy occasion when all could celebrate the goodness of God. Before all the guests went home the children sung them carols.

Again, the Secretaries told their testimony of what the Lord had done for them since coming to Sunderland and how they had been led to undertake the work with children. They acknowledged their dependence on the prayers of God's people and the need for the guidance of God in all they attempted to do.

Among the guests was Alexander who spoke of the considerable faith and courage of these two ladies who had taken on the responsibility not just of the house but in the training of the young girls. When this was reported in *Confidence* he appealed to all the readers to remember them in prayer.

Building on the Foundation

After leading in a prayer of thanksgiving, Alexander spoke an encouraging message from *Ephesians 2:20-22 (KJV)*, *'Built upon the foundation of the Apostles and Prophets, Jesus Christ himself being the chief cornerstone, in whom all the building, fitly framed together, groweth into an holy temple in the Lord; in whom ye are also builded together for an habitation of God, through the Spirit'*.

These two ladies were indeed building on the foundation laid in the parish by Alexander and Mary. Their growing home was a place where the Spirit of God was welcome.

A Call From God

It's not surprising that in July 1910 we read in *Confidence* that Margaret Howell and Mabel Scott announced their retirement from their secretarial work. The revival at Sunderland had increased the work load and it was time for changes to be made. Their work with children was obviously the main call on their lives and increasingly taking up their time.

There had apparently been some confusion in the minds of some people about who controlled the work of the 'Home'. The two ladies took this occasion to explain their call once again. They said, 'The plan and scope of this work was given us from the Lord and under Him we are carrying it out'. Alexander wanted it to be made clear that these ladies had heard from God and carried the responsibility and that he was in 'no way responsible for it'.

The ending of the secretarial duties released the ladies to take the children to Reeth in Yorkshire for a two month holiday. They asked that they may be witnesses for the Lord while there.

They Two Went On

On September 1st 1910 a meeting was held in Sunderland marking three years of the Pentecostal revival. It was full of testimonies and blessings of the last few years.

It was held in the Parish Hall and Margaret and Mabel were there with all their children. While in Reeth the Holy Spirit had baptised almost every member of their household. They were ready to begin a new chapter of the adventure which had become their new life in Sunderland. How apt that Alexander spoke on the text, *'They two went on'*, from *2 Kings 2:6 (KJV)*. He ended his talk by saying, 'Today we all need to go on...some have a dear friend or companion in Pentecost who encourages...They two go on'.

We hear nothing more of Miss Margaret Howell and Miss Mabel Scott and their happy band of children but there's no doubt they 'went on'. There's always more with God. Their work with these needy children was just one fruit of the revival as they captured something of the heart of God for the poor.

Full Of Faith And The Holy Spirit

Margaret and Mabel served God sacrificially. As the days in the Acts of the Apostles the number of disciples was increasing and people were needed to 'wait on tables' *(Acts 6:1-7)*. This they did faithfully and with integrity as they sent out the many copies of *Confidence*. Like Stephen, one of the first deacons, they too were full of faith and the Holy Spirit and God entrusted them with a successful ministry among the poor and with the children. It's a principle that as we are obedient and diligent God will increasingly entrust us with more of His work.

They were true *diakonoi*, servant hearted ministers who, doing what their hand found to do, responded to the call that God placed on their lives. Their call involved hard work. Sending out *Confidence* was hard work. The mission meetings among the poor were hard work. Looking after a household of twelve girls was hard work.

They were women who deserved honour and posthumously through this book we can expose their good deeds to a wider audience. I hope they are looking down from the grandstands of heaven and enjoying their moment.

Greet Margaret And Mabel

Paul wrote his list of greetings to the church at Rome. Among them were women who worked hard. He wrote,

> *'Greet Mary who worked very hard for you' (Romans 16:6)... 'Greet Tryphena and Tryphosa, those women who work hard in the Lord' (Romans 16:12)...'Greet my dear friend Persis, another woman who has worked very hard in the Lord' (Romans 16:12).*

How many, I wonder, would have added to their list of greetings to the church in Sunderland during those early years of the Pentecostal revival, 'Greet Margaret and Mabel, those women who work hard in the Lord'. I think there would be many.

---

1 Estrelda Alexander, *The Women of Azusa Street,* (Cleveland: The Pilgrim Press 2005), 51-55

9

Eleanor Crisp
Training A Generation

*'Everyone who comes to stay in the home will pass under
the rod, not only of direction and correction, but of
comfort of the Good Shepherd'*

Eleanor Crisp

Eleanor Crisp was the Principal of the Ladies' Testing and Training
Home for the Pentecostal Missionary Union for Great Britain and
Ireland (PMU). She exercised her authority from the time it opened in
January 1910 until its closure in 1922 with a brief period of retirement
in 1918. The young women who 'passed under the rod' came to love
and respect this strict disciplinarian whose love for the Lord and for
souls was the passion of her life. She moulded a generation of women
who gave themselves wholeheartedly to foreign missions.

She was also a sought after speaker at conventions not only in
London but in other parts of Britain. Her obituary, entitled *A Mother*

in Israel read, 'Wherever she went sinners were converted, Christians were blessed and the sick were healed. She had a wonderful insight into the Word of God, a comprehensive grasp of divine truth and a wide sympathy with all'.

Lydia Walshaw had been with her the week she died and said, 'How gifted she was! Her Bible talks, her gift of interpretation, her insight, discernment – so reliable, so sympathetic. She was just a darling'.

An Early Determination

Eleanor Searle was born in 1856 in Sidford Mills, Sidbury in the beautiful county of Devon. She was the youngest of seven children in the affluent Searle family. Her father, John, was a surveyor who had married her mother Caroline who was half his age. When Eleanor was born John was already sixty. What a trauma it must have been for Eleanor, when at the age of eleven the family moved from rural Devon to London.

She was saved just after the big move when she was twelve and for many years she was the only Christian in her family. Eleanor's decision to follow the Lord was a difficult one. Her determination, she said, 'separated her from some she dearly loved' and cost her 'loss of reputation, earthly joys and comforts'. But she had heard the call and obeyed His voice. Even as a young girl it seemed that whatever she put her hands to was blessed and the Sunday School and Bible Classes she taught grew in number.

When she was twenty one she married William Estcourt Crisp, a printer compositor in Bethnal Green. By the turn of the century she had given birth to seven daughters, Eleanor, Ethel, Daisy, Lily, May, Dorothy and Audrey. Her husband remains a mystery because he is never mentioned and I suspect she was widowed before her Pentecostal ministry became prominent. Eleanor would never have married someone who didn't share her beliefs and surely they would have ministered together in some way even if she did take a leading role. How did she support her family? Maybe an inheritance came to her from her wealthy family or from her husband.

Healed From Rheumatism

As a girl she had developed rheumatism which had such a crippling effect on her life that she found it difficult to turn even the pages of her Bible. Initially she had believed that sickness was chastisement from God and it took a Christian friend to point her to the scriptures which showed her it was the Lord's will to heal His people. To begin with she wasn't interested but began searching the Scriptures and later became convinced. She attended a local Church of England meeting in Hackney where many were healed as the vicar, John Allen, anointed them with oil. It was there that she was completely delivered and from then on she began a ministry of praying for the sick initially in that same church.

Eleanor then began to attend meetings at *Bethshan* in Highbury which had been established by William and Mary Boardman, Charlotte Murray and Elizabeth Baxter. The Boardmans had moved to London from the States in the 1880s teaching the doctrine of Healing in the Atonement and received by faith. Eventually a six hundred seater hall was needed for the Wednesday afternoon meetings on Holiness and Healing. We know that Eleanor took part in these meetings and used to be 'on the platform' so it's evident she played a prominent role.

A Lady Of Great Experience

When *Bethshan* closed she placed an advert in *The Christian Herald* newspaper asking that the many requests for prayer be sent to her personally. Sometimes she received two hundred letters a week and she prayed over every one no doubt assisted by her friend, Elizabeth Baxter who had been the guiding hand behind the home and also wife of the editor of *The Christian Herald*. Then the many answers to prayer were all published in the paper each week.

Around this time Eleanor opened a branch of the Young Women's Christian Association (YWCA) in Hackney which grew rapidly from half a dozen to over three hundred members. The weeks were full of Bible classes, prayer meetings and evangelistic services. Many were converted and blessed at these gatherings. She placed a great emphasis on missions and from time to time girls offered themselves for the foreign mission field some of whom later joined the PMU. Later one missionary in China wrote, '[I] was led to the YWCA where Mrs. Crisp presided and found there a red hot missionary spirit. [I] was born again and had subsequently a mighty Baptism in the Spirit. The call came 'Will you be a missionary?'' Her own daughter, Audrey, later went as a missionary to Africa.

Eleanor was quick to embrace the Pentecostal message of the Baptism of the Holy Spirit with the accompanying sign of tongues. Already a Holiness teacher and a believer in a 'second blessing' she was open to receive the gift of tongues.

Given her track record, it is no surprise that Eleanor Crisp was asked to be the principal of the first Pentecostal Testing and Training Home for Ladies. Alexander Boddy called her, 'A baptised lady of great experience'. She willingly took on this role and initially managed to carry on with all her other activities as well. She was supported by all her daughters and occasionally they helped her at the home.

Salvation's Story Telling

The opening of the Ladies' Training Home in January 1910 followed the opening of the Men's Home in Paddington the July of the previous year. The home was at 116 King Edward Road, South Hackney, London and it had the capacity to hold twelve women.

Both homes opened to train men and women who were baptised in the Holy Spirit and had heard the missionary call. The emphasis of the early Pentecostal Movement was on foreign mission and a training programme for those at home was not considered a necessity believing the Holy Spirit was teacher enough and it was the 'heathen' that needed to be reached. The home was the brain child of Cecil Polhill, President of the PMU, who had seen the liability untrained missionaries were on the field and was determined this was not going to happen with those sent out by the PMU.

Eleanor was in charge of all household arrangements and had, 'under divine direction', furnished the four storied house. She had a lady who helped her, a Miss Shepherd, whose job was specified as 'house mother'. Eleanor didn't live at the home but nearby at 19 Gascoyne Road, South Hackney. The home was described as 'clean and trim'. Eleanor had only bought what was necessary and no money had been wasted, probably because there wasn't any to waste but also knowing the hardships missionaries face no doubt she thought it was a good idea to introduce a spartan existence early on to separate the wheat from the chaff. Texts for the walls and an organ or piano were still needed and Eleanor appealed to those present at the opening to give something for the home.

While Miss Shepherd was preparing tea in the basement kitchen for the guests, the opening ceremony was taking place upstairs. Cecil Polhill led the meeting and Alexander Boddy read from the Bible. There were many guests including Catherine Price whose 'Home of Rest' in Brixton was used for prayer meetings. Eleanor set the standard in her no nonsense address to the assembled gathering. 'Everyone who comes to stay in the home will pass under the rod, not only of direction and correction, but of comfort of the Good Shepherd'.

It ended with them all singing the hymn which told of the reason for their existence,

> Far, far away in heathen darkness dwelling,
> Millions of souls forever may be lost;
> Who, who will go, salvation's story telling,
> Looking to Jesus, counting not the cost?

Faith In God Is The Capital

Eleanor believed she had a call from God for this work and that it was her privilege to serve in this way. This she did willingly and wholeheartedly.

The home operated entirely on faith principles and no one received any salary including herself. The PMU made it clear they weren't responsible for any student support, maintenance or expenses either in the Training Home or in the foreign field. As freewill offerings were given to the PMU, the council distributed the money first to the missionaries abroad and then to the home.

We know that in 1911 the home needed £20 a month to operate and funds were often in short supply. At one missionary meeting at a Sunderland Convention, Eleanor spoke from *2 Corinthians 9:6* on the law of sowing and reaping. She concluded,

> 'Faith in God, therefore, is the principle upon which we work. Faith in God is the capital and God gives the increase. We are not in debt to anyone except 'the debt of love' and we have no reserves'.

Letters from the missionaries telling of their financial hardships overshadowed the needs of the home and Eleanor was not slow in championing the cause. As the only woman on the PMU council she argued for reduced fees for foreign students and won her case. In 1910 the fees were duly halved to five shillings a week.

'Jerkers' And 'Shirkers'

A report in *Confidence* regarding the home said it was started with the object of 'testing and training young women'. Eleanor taught the books of the Bible from Genesis to Revelation and set herself the task of developing the character of the women students. At the opening ceremony she said,

> 'He is calling the base and foolish and ignorant; but the Holy Ghost is the illuminator. The knowledge of the Word comes by real work, though then the Spirit illuminates. Some become 'jerkers' and afterwards 'shirkers'. All mere learning for learning's sake is avoided. Soul winners should be taught to win souls...After the first month the ladies will give Gospel addresses and deal with souls'.

All enough to make any would be missionary quake in their shoes and return home if she were not certain of her calling.

Looking Back Over The First Year

So what happened on a day to day basis? Let Eleanor tell us in a report she gave about the home which was in the March 1911 edition of *Confidence*.

> 'The chief work at the home is a systematic study of the Scriptures under the light and teaching of the Holy Spirit. This is found to be increasingly interesting, and will, we are sure, prove of the greatest value to students in their future work. A considerable time is also allotted each day for definite, intercessory prayer. In addition to this lessons are also given in English, Geography and the peoples and religions of the world, the last three being a considerable aid to intelligent prayer for all nations'.

At the home Eleanor had put big maps on the wall to help with intercession. She also continued to receive as many as forty requests for prayer a week which she gave to her students to pray over. She said these brought 'great blessing to those who send the requests and those who pray'. Her report continued,

> 'A written test is given weekly bearing on the subject matter taken during the week. We also have two harmoniums... and on these the students who have not already learned are taught to play hymns, and as far as lies in their power, to sing. [Singing was a key evangelistic tool on the mission field to gather a crowd.]
>
> Besides their studies the students have the privilege of helping at various women's meetings in the neighbourhood. These are of such diverse kinds that it gives them the opportunity of dealing with Christians and unbelievers both old and young, and we believe much blessing has been the result.
>
> A tarrying meeting is held at the home every Monday from 7.30 to 10 pm and we know of many who have received definite blessing. We do, indeed, praise God with our hearts for all that He has done among us.
>
> As we look back over our first year, we can indeed say that

> God has been with us of a truth; our hearts have burned within us as He has talked with us by the way, and has opened to us the Scriptures. What the Holy Spirit has taught us direct from the Word and by means of His gifts, will, we trust remain in our hearts when far separated one from the other. To Him be all the glory. Hallelujah!'

It seems, too, that the students had favour in their immediate neighbourhood. They did house to house visitation and were often invited into the homes of the people to read and pray with the sick. They were always welcomed at the various chapels near the home as well. One lady commented it was because there was 'life in their messages'. They worked among young people and helped in prayer meetings for the sick. They were kept busy. Mrs. Crisp would not allow 'shirkers'!

Lessons were also given in elocution 'for clear speaking and enunciation' obviously thought essential in these days of Empire over and above learning the languages of the countries where they were to serve. However, Eleanor regarded anything that was not studying the Bible, prayer or other overtly Christian work as a 'side study' and she said, 'Although we don't put a great value on these side studies, yet we believe God should have the best as far as we are concerned'.

Shaping Lives

Many sought her advice on different matters, both men and women but especially those in the Ladies' Training Home.

By March 1911 there were seven ladies in training. Four had left and were already in India and two were on their way. The Beruldsen girls, Christina and Thyra were in China. The propriety of the age made it necessary for all missionaries to have suitable clothing and Eleanor saw to this herself, personally selecting their outfits which were paid for out of PMU funds. Chapter Ten, *Missionary Ladies*, traces the fortunes of some of the young women once they had been moulded by Eleanor Crisp.

At a valedictory meeting at Sion College, London in March 1914 five women who were about to sail to China gave their parting message. Although a rather formidable figure, their appreciation and affection for Eleanor is evident.

Miss Fanny Jenner said, 'It has been a wonderful ten years [she had been at the YWCA] since I was bought into contact with Mrs. Crisp. She never wanted me to lean on *her*, and when she found I was doing it, she threw me off on to the Lord. Sometimes this seemed hard'.

Another, Miss Ida de Vries commented, 'Mrs. Crisp has been a great blessing to me,' and Miss Maggie Millar said, 'I praise God for all Mrs. Crisp has been led to do for the development of my character'.

The leaders of the meeting laid hands on them and off they went to China. Just a few of the many young women whose lives were 'shaped' by this godly, yet strict disciplinarian.

The Uplifted Eye

This was the title of an address Eleanor gave at the Sunderland Convention in 1914 and it was printed in *Confidence*. It shows the esteem with which Eleanor was held that she was invited to be the key speaker at such prestigious events. Her talk was based on *John 4:35 (KJV)*, '*Say not ye, there are four months and then cometh harvest? Behold, I say unto you, Lift up your eyes and look on the fields; for they are white already to harvest*'. The following extracts illustrate her passion for missions.

> 'I'm never so glad as when I'm sending people out to the Mission Field. With all my heart I could cry over them, but at the same time I could shout with joy. I tell all those who go down to the railway terminus at Tilbury Dock: 'Now don't go down there and take any tears; shed your tears at home; then you will be able to bear them up and encourage them!' And there is such a mixture of feelings, because I see myself that we are just landing another one out there – another filled with the Holy Ghost. I used to be glad twenty years ago but not in the same way, because our missionaries are now going baptised with the Holy Ghost,

and with this blessing they know that God will heal the sick; they know that the Lord will work with them. The Lord is the secret of their power, and will confirm the Word with signs following'.

She didn't let those off who stayed at home. Home or away the same commitment was required.

'If only Pentecostal people saw their privilege – to look unto the fields, to the central parts of Africa! We know how people there are crying out for God and asking for teachers. There are only certain ones that can go out, but we can all lift up our eyes and those who go out need those on fire at home who can pray through for them'.

She ended by challenging those present that if they just looked, 'lifted up their eyes', they would see the wonderful opportunities all around them. She believed that people or 'souls' as she put it, wanted to be won. All we needed to do was to come alongside them as Jesus did with the woman at the well not to 'scold them' or 'drive them' or 'pelt them with texts'. 'We will never get a revival,' she said, 'Until we know how to win souls'.

She Inspired Confidence

Eleanor was a frequent speaker at Pentecostal Conferences around the country. We read of her speaking at the annual Sunderland Conventions until they ceased at the time of the First World War and then continued at Kingsway Hall in London where she regularly ministered. She shared platforms in Edinburgh, Bradford and Belfast with such well known figures as George Jeffreys and Smith Wigglesworth. She toured round Pentecostal works and her reports are recorded in *Confidence*.

Writing about Eleanor, Pentecostal leader Donald Gee said, 'She seemed to radiate competency. To see her on the platform of a Pentecostal Convention was enough to inspire confidence...she always wore a neat blue bonnet and was the essence of modesty'.[1]

Eleanor was an excellent teacher of the Word. Her sermons were always delivered with great clarity and showed her spiritual wisdom and insight. She was not afraid of tackling books such as Ezekiel and Revelation always bringing a relevant message to challenge her hearers.

Many of her sermons were printed almost in full in various issues of *Confidence*. In talks on the book of *Jude* and *Corinthians* she addresses the use of spiritual gifts and various other issues in the church offering not just her thoughts but correction and direction. Her forthrightness would have caused many to sit up and take note. This woman spoke godly common sense which it seems was accepted and applauded by all.

She is an example of just one of many women who exercised a strong teaching gift in mixed gatherings in the early years of the Pentecostal Movement. Her obituary, written in a 1924 edition of *Confidence* said, 'Her messages always from the Word of God, were like breezes from the ocean of His love and many can testify that she taught them the secret of a happy life'.

Not Wish-bones But Back-bones

Eleanor Crisp had a practical, no nonsense approach to life. In one sermon she said, 'The Holy Spirit required not wish-bones but back-bones!' She was a hard worker and didn't suffer fools gladly. Her name suited her!

She was a lady who was full of the power of the Holy Spirit and once likened herself to a motor car. 'I am just like a motor car when it is stopped but when the brake is off, I can go'. She worked along side her male colleagues on the PMU Council who held her in just a little awe as did the 'brothers' in The Men's Training Home. She was a woman of sound judgement and her spiritually practical approach caused her to be sought after time and again when difficulties arose. When it came to a matter of guidance some were relying on tongues and interpretation rather than getting on their knees and seeking God. In her distinct way she called this, 'A lazy bit of business'.

Dingalala

So in the light of that it is surprising that Eleanor herself exercised a remarkable gift of the interpretation of tongues. She used this gift on many public occasions. A wonderful story is told from the1913 Sunderland Convention. There had been a message in tongues and the language was recognized by a missionary and a linguist who was present, a Miss Alma Doering from Congo. She identified the language as being spoken by the Kifioti tribe. The message in tongues began with a peculiar cry, 'Dingalala, dingalala', which she said was the way this tribe made a call to attention before giving an important message.

As the message in tongues was being given, Miss Doering whispered the interpretation to a man sitting next to her on the platform. Then Eleanor, sitting a distance away, gave the interpretation. When she reached the part of the message which Miss Doering had understood, it was exactly the same as the interpretation she whispered to the man next to her. This story was even reported in the *London Daily News*.

A Practical Gift

She did, not unsurprisingly, see the practical side of speaking of tongues. She voiced the hope that those training for foreign fields would be given the gift of languages or help them with 'easy acquirement' so that the Gospel message might be carried far and wide. Unfortunately letters from missionaries sent out by the PMU tell of having to learn foreign languages the hard way although there were remarkable incidences of the languages being recognisable in the early years of the Pentecostal Movement.

At a missionary meeting in 1911 she again spoke of the practical instruction tongues and interpretation can bring when praying. She comments, 'Several pages could be filled in telling how God is using the gift of tongues and interpretation...In intercession we have been taken over all countries...This is not in addition to the Word of God but an opening out of it in a most practical way...Praying in tongues in your own room is not wasted, you are making intercession according to the will of God'. She was a believer that the Pentecostal blessing gave them power to pray as they had never prayed before.

She also knew that tongues was a gift from God given for the 'building up [of] your most holy faith' *(Jude 20)*. Tongues was a gift that she used in the private of her own room rather than in a public setting. It was alone with God that she spoke 'as much as ever the Lord wants me to speak'. She said, 'It just bubbles up. When my mind is all upon God, He gives me glorious visions of the Lord in glory. And sometimes He takes me up in the Spirit and I am with Him. I have been in heaven with God many times'.

Made Holy

The addresses of these early Pentecostal ladies frequently reveal contemporary thought, as would be expected. Speaking at the London Convention of 1915, Eleanor taught on how to enter into *The Victorious Life*. It's interesting that she is still teaching the idea that a single act of 'full surrender' of a believer produces 'entire sanctification'.

This was the Holiness teaching which equated the Baptism in the Holy Spirit with being made holy. A union in the death of Christ meant a union in His risen life so it was possible for a believer to be 'saved above sin, saved from the power of the enemy, [and] saved from self,' enabling them to 'live a life that will keep [them] sweet and beautiful all the time'.

'Holiness' she said, 'Is a real act of God on our hearts and lives'.

A Little Bit Of Fence

In 1917 she addressed a gathering of Pentecostals at Kingsway Hall, London where she taught from the book of *Corinthians*. She spoke about the different issues this first century church was facing and it's interesting to see how she applied them to the early Pentecostal Movement in Britain.

The following extract as printed in *Confidence* gives us an insight into the two camps that were developing. She spoke from *1 Corinthians 3* regarding divisions in the church because they were following different leaders. She said that 'in some Pentecostal circles people are claiming to be more blessed under certain teachers'. Her talk continued,

> 'There are Pentecostal people today who encourage separation. It seems that the little bit of fence between us is like the little fence running through the London gardens, you can look over one another's fence and enjoy the sight of one another's gardens. There are no divisions in Pentecost. 'He hath broken down the middle wall of division'.
>
> There used to be divisions and there was no unity between Church of England people and Baptists, but we are on the same platform today. I am thankful to know that the dividing walls are broken down if we are in Pentecostal circles. That there is a little bit of fence I agree. In your own London garden you have a little fence to save it from the neighbour's dog and other things but that fence does not prevent the air or the sunshine or the rain coming, it does not shut out any of the good things of God, which are all free.
>
> The Holy Ghost when He came down did not stop to see if I was a Baptist or Churchwoman. He came from God and baptised me, just as I was, a member of the Baptist body; and He can baptise you in the same way. Pastor Boddy is in the Church of England; others are Baptists. Some have their own mission but all can meet in a Pentecostal gathering. There is that little bit of fence because it is better for the working out of the whole, for we can all work in our own place which God has allotted to us'.

I wonder if this had some of those present squirming in their seats! But this early ecumenical attitude was soon to be challenged as the Pentecostal Movement became formalised denominationally.

Elderly Babes

Then in her forthright manner she turned to address gullible Christians who, though baptised in the Holy Spirit, were not able to handle the Word of God correctly and feed themselves with solid food *(1 Corinthians 3:2)*.

She calls them elderly babes who are still on milk. Hitting home the point she remarked, 'That has been part of the trouble in our Pentecostal assemblies. People have come along preaching some remarkable truth which they have got in some portion of Scripture and they teach it as if it were the whole of the truth specially revealed and the babes suck it all down as such'. Such wisdom would not go amiss today.

A Scriptural Revival

We glean another interesting insight when she relates her views regarding the Welsh Revival which was at that time only a decade old. During the years 1904-5 one fifth of the population of Wales had come to Christ as the Holy Spirit had moved powerfully through the valleys. Speaking in 1915 she comments,

> 'It is said by some that the reason that the Welsh Revival did not go on was it was not a revival according to the Word of God but because of the brokenness of His servants. As they stood forth the Spirit of God swept through the great gatherings, and the people were broken down. His servants sometimes only spoke a word or two and the Spirit worked in the meetings in a wonderful way and many precious souls were blessed'.

Whilst not denigrating in any way the work of the Spirit, she said what was needed was 'A Scriptural Revival', a balance of the work of the Word and Spirit. 'Let our prayer be,' she pleaded, *'Lord, revive me according to your Word' (Psalm 119:156)*. 'What we need…is a mighty quickening according to the Word of God'.

The Tip Top Of Expectation

Like all early Pentecostals Eleanor believed that she would live to see the return of the Lord. According to the teaching of the time, the outpouring of the Holy Spirit with the sign of tongues put their generation in the prophetic time frame of the latter rain. A time when the end time harvest would be bought in and mark the end of the age. There were also many prophetic words and apocalyptic messages given fuelled by the unrest in Europe and the subsequent World War. So it is not a surprise when she voiced these words in 1913,

> 'I expect to live to see the day when He shall come. I am looking for His coming every morning and every evening. My soul is always on the tip top of expectation and when I look at the stars I think, 'He may be coming before morning'.

And in 1917, the eminently practical Eleanor Crisp said, 'I am making no provision for my funeral, for my burial place. I am not looking that way but the other way. He is coming'.

Time For A Rest

An announcement appeared in *Confidence* (April-June 1918),

> 'The PMU have suffered a great loss in the retiring (at any rate for a time) of Mrs. Crisp from the training home, of which she has so long and efficiently acted as principal. Mrs. Crisp has long felt the urgent need of a rest from her exacting duties of which the training home was only a part. We desire to place on record our grateful appreciation of Mrs. Crisp's earnest and able work in the training, and her influence on the lives of many, both now in preparation and on the mission field. We wish her a full restoration of vitality and strength; and in the meantime are happy to know that we still retain Mrs. Crisp's presence to help on the council'.

A Miss Morrell became her successor and the home moved to 7 Eton Road, Haverstock Hill in Hampstead. Even though she was sixty two, retirement doesn't come easily to people like Eleanor and in 1919 she is referred to as 'the Superintendent of the Home' and by 1920 she once again appears as 'The Lady Principal'. Unfortunately by 1922 both the men's and ladies' homes had to close for a while because of the PMU's financial difficulties. The two homes jointly reopened in 1923 under the leadership of Howard Carter.

A Scarred Warrior

Three weeks before her death she had a speaking engagement in Croydon. Her text was *2 Peter 1:11 (KJV) 'For so an entrance shall be ministered to you abundantly into the everlasting kingdom of our Lord and Saviour Jesus Christ'*. She said she would rather go home a scarred warrior than not go home a warrior at all, but that she desired not to enter glory a battered wreck but to have an 'abundance entrance' bringing her sheaves with her. She still had speaking engagements a week before she died and to the end she attended the PMU council meetings even though she looked 'tired and worn'.

Donald Gee knew Eleanor and he relates a conversation he had with her in her latter years. She told him, 'Twenty years ago I felt I could reasonably expect about twenty more years for active life and service. So I asked the Lord to pack as much as He could into the next twenty years...And I think He had done so'.

Eleanor Crisp went to be with the Lord on October 16th 1923. She was sixty eight years old. Eleanor had been suffering from valvular heart disease and then developed pneumonia. She died at the home of her daughter Ethel Titterington in Bromley, Kent.

In her memory the PMU council planned to raise money to build a hall for the preaching of the full Gospel in Hackney which had been her home for many years, a place where she had been blessed and was a blessing to so many. There were still some young people there in the now struggling YWCA and it was felt to be a fitting way to remember this dear woman who had given her life to serve a generation. Sadly I can find no evidence that it was ever built.

Holding Court

Alexander Boddy called Eleanor Crisp a 'Mother in Israel' and she was certainly a mother to many holding court not under a palm tree *(Judges 4:5)* but at the Ladies' Testing and Training Home in Hackney!

Although some of her stern ways and inflexible attitudes are foreign to our present generation we have to understand Eleanor as a woman of her time. We need to look past the rather formidable exterior to the heart which was soft and tender before the Lord. It is such a one that He uses.

There is no doubting that this lady poured her life into a generation who took the Gospel to the ends of the earth first in the YWCA and then at the Training Home. She took this work seriously in the sincere belief that Jesus was coming back soon and that the Holy Spirit had been outpoured with the gift of tongues for that very purpose.

We would call it 'discipleship'. She called it 'passing under the rod'. The results were the same, young women who developed their own secure walk with the Lord. She shared with them the insights she gleaned from personal Bible study and from her intimate times with her Saviour. To paraphrase *Acts 18:26*, like Pricilla, she invited them into her home and explained to them the way of God more adequately.

The book of Psalms especially is full of verses which encourage us to speak of the works of God from one generation to another. David wrote about this in *Psalm 145:4-7 'One generation commends Your works to another...They speak of the glorious splendour of Your majesty...They tell of the power of Your awesome works...They will celebrate Your abundant goodness and joyfully sing of Your righteousness'.*

Like Eleanor, we still need to live in the light of Jesus' return and make it our priority to train a generation to take the Gospel to those who haven't heard whether they be in the inner cities or Irian Jaya.

Failing to do that would be 'A lazy bit of business'. I let Eleanor Crisp have the last word as I'm sure she always did.

---

1 For this and other comments see Donald Gee, *These Men I Knew,* (Nottingham: AOG Publishing House, 1980), 34-35

10

Betty Jones and Grace Elkington

Missionary Ladies
They Paid A Price

'In most cases when a girl gives herself to God
for foreign service, it is all she has to give'

Eleanor Crisp

From our 21st century perspective we can only stand back and wonder at the young women who were willing to risk their lives taking the Gospel to the remotest parts of our world. They faced hardships, sickness and some died on foreign fields. All of them had one thing in common, the love for their Saviour and Lord and love for the multitudes who had never heard the good news of the Gospel. Each one deserves a chapter to themselves but together they are the 'Missionary Ladies' who were willing to pay the price of a life wholly given to God.

Go! Go! Go!

This was the rallying cry at conventions. Seen as a natural fruit of Pentecost, young hearts were being set on fire to minister in 'dark heathen lands'. The latter rain was falling for the speedy evangelisation of the nations. As in the book of *Acts* people were once again speaking in new tongues. It was the midnight hour. Time was short. Jesus was coming back, maybe, as had been prophesied, in 1914. Scriptures such as, *'This Gospel of the kingdom will be preached in the whole world as a testimony to all nations, and then the end will come' (Matthew 24:14)* were set in sharp focus.

So the sacrifice of these women needs to be put in a context of apocalyptic fervour fuelled by a prophetic time frame. Pentecostal historian, Vinson Synan called them 'Missionaries of the one way ticket'[1] because many never expected to see home shores again. More generally the British missionary endeavour had been increasing for the past one hundred years and was to climax in the Edinburgh Missionary Conference of 1910 which boasted one thousand two hundred international delegates.

The heroes of the day were those who rose to the challenge like mill worker Gladys Eaton whose departure from the Welsh valleys for training before going to China was captured in this romanticised scene. 'All the young girls of the mill went up the road a little way to meet her and flock round her and... [they] escorted their spiritual hero to the train and there on the platform our dear sister told them once again of the wonderful Gospel'.

Monday, Study Chinese

Initially the tongues were perceived to be actual languages *(xenolalia)* given by the Holy Spirit to bypass the arduous task of learning a foreign language. If the language could be identified then the missionary would know the country to which he or she were called. This was especially the belief in the early days of the outpouring at Azusa Street in America, 1906, when various ones sailed off to foreign lands only to find that the indigenous populations didn't understand them.

As early as 1908 Alexander Boddy, gracious as ever, said that even so God honoured their zeal and blessed their endeavours but commented, 'As far as I can see [God] will not use that means to convert the heathen'.

I'm sure that many missionaries wished He would because once in their place of calling they had to spend many laborious hours of language study. Desperate to tell the good news about Jesus this proved very frustrating. One missionary wrote home in honesty, 'Monday, study Chinese, Tuesday, doing the same, Wednesday, item, and so on until Saturday, week after week, month after month; but it is indeed a great trial'.

Having said that there have been incidences where actual languages were recognized but usually in a prophetic utterance rather than a continuous fluent language and these were exceptions rather than the rule. Many missionary addresses were still peppered with the hope that God would give complete languages.

We do hear of some missionaries who rejected language study as 'human' and just screamed and shouted in tongues bringing the movement into disrepute, but none of our missionary ladies did that. Every month in *Confidence* letters contained heartfelt requests for prayer: 'May the Lord make it easy and shorten the time'.

Supernatural Outfit

Rather than just the emphasis on tongues, missionaries were encouraged to exercise the Gifts of the Spirit in their mission field. Ever astute, Alexander said at one missionary meeting, 'The Lord needs today, missionaries, men and women in the apostolic succession with apostolic equipment – the Gifts of the Spirit – men who in His name shall lay hands on the sick and they shall recover, who in that almighty name shall cast out demons and they shall go'. He called this their supernatural outfit which was indispensable if their work was to succeed.

He challenged them with the story of a polite Chinaman who said, 'Your Lord Jesus is wonderful but why does he not do any of these things through you today?' Authenticity, then as now, must be at the heart of the Gospel.

The Ends Of The Earth

Jesus said, *'But you shall receive power when the Holy Spirit comes on you; and you will be My witnesses in Jerusalem, and in all Judea and Samaria, and to the ends of the earth' (Acts 1:8).*

The first wave of women who responded to the call went to India and China. Many had never left the relative safety of the British Isles and in those days of the Empire any place which had not embraced western civilization was described as 'dark' and 'heathen'. This was captured in the favourite missionary hymn of the day, 'Far, Far away in heathen darkness dwelling...'

You couldn't get more 'ends of the earth' than the borders of Tibet. This Buddhist country high in the Himalayas was described as, 'The land of seclusion and mystery; of vast plains and immense altitudes; the last country to open its doors to the world's commerce, or to the messenger of the Gospel.' Maybe because of what it represented but more probably because the China Inland Mission (CIM), which was founded by Hudson Taylor in 1865, were poised in Yunnan Province on the Tibetan borders ready for when the doors were opened.

Since the 1880s Cecil Polhill, with a group of Cambridge graduates called The Cambridge Seven had worked in China as a missionary with the CIM. After receiving his Baptism in the Spirit in 1908 at a friend's house in Los Angeles the day after visiting Azusa, Polhill joined Boddy in setting up the Pentecostal Missionary Union (PMU) and China was a mission field that was already known and close to his heart.

Mukti

Frank Bartleman, a chronicler of the Pentecostal Revival, said it was 'bought up in India', meaning that prior to the Azusa outpouring there was a revival in India that straddled the years 1905-7. It all started at *Mukti Mission*, a home for young widows and orphans near Poona (Pune), one hundred miles south of Bombay. In the Marathi language *'Mukti'* means freedom, liberation and salvation and the mission still cares for the poor and needy today. A converted Brahmin woman, Pandita Ramabai founded the work in 1899 and challenged by the Welsh

Revival encouraged her girls to pray for revival in India. By June 1905, five hundred and fifty girls were meeting twice a day for prayer.

The Lord answered by fire, literally! The girls had prayed that they might be filled with the Holy Spirit. One night at 3.30am one girl woke up with 'fire coming down on her'. She screamed as the other girls watched the flames. The girls' matron rushed in and was about to throw a bucket of water on her when she discovered she was not burning. Other girls experienced tongues of fire coming upon them, some saw visions of Jesus and had angelic visitations. There was much weeping and confession of sin. Many came from across India to see for themselves as the news spread. Thousands of these young women were trained as evangelists and travelled to the surrounding villages taking the Gospel.

The events surrounding this revival were well known to British Pentecostals. Collections were made for the widows and letters from an American missionary, Minnie Abrams, who worked with Pandita were printed in *Confidence*. In 1908/9 Minnie and Manoramabai, Pandita's daughter visited Britain. So it is no surprise that some of first women missionaries from Britain went to India and made *Mukti* their initial destination.

The PMU And The Call

In order for missionaries to be sent to foreign fields the Pentecostal Missionary Union for Great Britain and Ireland was established at a meeting in Sunderland on January 9th 1909. Governed by an executive council with a general council of seventeen local representatives, fund raising missionary boxes were distributed and support groups established. Pentecostal leaders were encouraged to send their very best workers. Part of the PMU's prayer went like this,

> 'O Lord give us a heart of love for the heathen in Asia, Africa, America and the Islands of the Sea...Show us each one what we may do, and give us grace to do it as unto thee. Chose Thine own messengers and may none of us refuse to hear a call...'

The missionary 'call' was an important concept. A missionary to Congo, Alma Doering, clarified what this meant in a message she gave to a missionary meeting at Sunderland.

'To have strong, deep sympathies and intense yearnings towards those in heathen darkness and depravity should be the normal state of those who have anything of Christ's tender heart of compassion, but fervent sympathies do not make a call to go'.

She said there were three necessities, the Word of God spoken into the inner being. Secondly, the response in the heart to the Spirit and the witness of outward circumstances. The women who gave themselves for missionary service were encouraged to testify to a definite call which acted as a means of self validation.

Testing And Training

A call alone does not a missionary make. Veteran missionary, Polhill, admitted that he had seen mistakes made in sending out unprepared workers who were 'full of zeal but lacking in knowledge of the Word'.

As we already noted when we looked at the life of Eleanor Crisp, a decision was taken at the Sunderland Convention 1909 to open a 'Training and Testing Home'. From January 1910 onwards, training and testing took place under the hawk eyes of Mrs. Crisp. If they 'survived' Mrs. Crisp and the rigours of the Training Home then there was a good chance they would survive on the mission field!

All candidates considered for training had to be baptised in the Holy Spirit with accompanying 'signs and gifts'. On leaving, 'They must have a fair knowledge of every book of the Bible and an accurate knowledge of the doctrines of Salvation and Sanctification'. Weekly tests kept them on their toes.

Ladies who didn't make the grade were weeded out under the 'rod of correction and direction'. They stayed in the home until they were considered 'ripe for service abroad, no longer'. Then at their valedictory meeting they were presented with a 'Certificate of the Union'. Money then had to be raised for their passages to their countries of destination and for their outfits which was in those days considered a very necessary part of the sending process.

Even though from a 21st century perspective there were gaps in the curriculum such as elocution lessons being favoured over language study. After one of his visits to missionaries in the field Polhill was able to say that 'All our women missionaries bear emphatic testimony to the great help received in Bible training through their stay at Hackney' and I'm sure they did.

It Is All She Has To Give

In keeping with the philosophy of the CIM, the PMU was a faith mission only guaranteeing board and clothing. Eleanor Crisp began this training at the home explaining, 'In most cases when a girl gives herself to God for foreign service, it is all she has to give, so of necessity, she has to begin at once with us to exercise faith in God for her supplies'.

On the home front, the choir boys and women's Bible study group at Sunderland, the Hackney YWCA, Lydia Walshaw's missionary band, Emmaus and countless other groups faithfully collected money in the missionary boxes. Applications for the boxes always rose when a 'real live missionary' told romantic tales of far off lands. Before returning to India, Margaret Clarke spoke at Sunderland in 1910.

Confidence records, 'She took us into the crowded streets of Bombay, by day and by night...We went into the jungle country and learnt something of the difficulties and discomforts from insect life, abounding and merciless, almost more than the snakes, scorpions, centipedes, jackals and possibly tigers. We learnt of the hearts here and there yearning for God's best, and the heroism of faith in cases where persecution was so real and overwhelming'. Following this, Margaret was fortunate when an anonymous donor pledged £60 a year. This lady had always hoped to be a missionary herself, Margaret was to be her 'substitute'.

From Our Own Missionary

And so they went and wrote their letters home. In *Confidence* letters 'From our own Missionaries' took pride of place each month and they were read out at missionary meetings and conventions. They told of dangers and victories, revolutions and revivals and what every day life was like in these far away places, no doubt hoping to touch purses as well as hearts. One delightfully honest missionary wrote of the temptation to 'look through the coloured glasses of expectancy and announce the birth already' sending reports home that will satisfy the expectation of friends.

Sometimes the exploits read like the female equivalent of the old 'Boy's Own' comics and one can imagine the readers waiting with bated breath for next month's instalment of life on Tibet's border or what happened when the single missionary with the widows from *Mukti* encountered a mob armed with sticks who were threatening their lives. An amateur photographer himself, Alexander encouraged them to send in photos which he printed in *Confidence*. Thereafter appeared images which bought the foreign fields and their inhabitants to life. Some were sad like the missionary family standing round a coffin of their child on a Chinese hillside. Others show the British women dressed in Chinese clothes outside Chinese homes. Then there were the stereotypical missionary photos of ladies dressed in European clothes wearing pith helmets surrounded by natives or in simple white frocks in their Indian bungalows.

Whoever the missionary and wherever the work, there was always the cry for more workers acknowledging that the *'harvest is plentiful but the workers are few' (Luke 10:2)*.

Ripe For Going Forth

Miss Lucy James of Bedford and Miss Kathleen Millar of Exeter go down in Pentecostal history as the first two missionaries sent out by the PMU in February 1909. According to Cecil Polhill there was no shortage of volunteers but these sisters were the only ones who were 'ripe for going forth' without training. Kathleen Miller had already spent six years in India and spoke Tamil and Bengali.

Initially they both went to *Mukti* and began writing letters home about the revival amongst the girls. After a short period in the hills during the hot season, a mission field in itself among missionaries sceptical of the sign of 'tongues', Lucy returned to *Mukti* and Kathleen to Bombay. Here she helped Miss Maud Orlebar who ran a 'Home of Rest' called *Beulah*. Ironically Maud died the next year because 'she was just worn out'.

Lucy continued with language study and itinerated round the villages with the widows from *Mukti* using Bible Women, trained nationals who acted as interpreters and teachers for the missionaries. They would often go for months at a time and live in tents in unevangelised territories. One of the means of gathering a crowd was to sing hymns accompanied by a small organ they had bought with them. It would seem too that Lucy was very gifted in giving messages in tongues and interpretation.

Life in foreign climes took its toll and in 1912 Lucy found herself seriously ill in hospital in Poona. Able to recover enough to go back to England for a rest she returned to India confident of her calling to the villages. Based in Faizpur some two hundred miles inland from Bombay, she was joined by PMU missionary Lucy Wakeford and wrote home in 1914,

> 'The work is wonderful; we go to a village and everybody turns out to see us and then we preach. The people seem to forget everything and just sit and drink in the Gospel message like truly thirsty souls; they will sit for hours and never seem to tire'.

The Ultimate Price

After her stay with Maud, Kathleen went to Cuttack on the east coast where she saw a similar revival to that at *Mukti* at the girls' school and orphanage where she was staying. Children and teachers alike were being saved, sanctified and filled with the Holy Spirit. In one letter she wrote, 'Words can't describe the wonderful things I have seen here the last day or two. It is now only 9am and I have just come from the school room where thirty five girls are on their faces on the floor before God…'

Sadly, the next time we hear of Kathleen is in the column *Pentecostal Items*, in the December 1911 edition of *Confidence*. 'We have recently received tidings from India of the home call of…our beloved friend, Miss Kathleen Miller, who for some time has been living with a native Christian lady in Bengal, but has not been strong of late'. She paid the ultimate price.

Sisters Of The Union

The ensuing years saw young women trained at the London Training Home and sent out to India as proud holders of the Certificate of the Union. In early 1911 Miss Margaret Clarke, a seasoned missionary to India, sailed with Miss Constance Skarratt followed by Miss Grace Elkington who had been born in India and Miss Betty Jones. Margaret and Grace spoke various Indian languages and so were able to help the others with language study.

No reading novels and enjoying the sunshine on deck, on their voyage to Bombay they had Bible studies in Revelation and Ezekiel! After a period of settling in at *Mukti*, Margaret and Constance began a Pentecostal Mission in Jalna further inland. From there they travelled around the villages sleeping in tents which became unbearable when temperatures rose to 106 degrees. It's no wonder that Margaret had a severe attack of sun fever.

They wrote in 1912, 'The whole field lies open before us, villages and towns of those who do not know God'. Working with three native evangelists who were supported at £10 a year from Britain and one Bible Woman, they would often hold three meetings a day when men, women and children came from distances of twenty miles.

On The Move

Every time news was received from Margaret and Constance they were talking about moving forward into fresh fields. While at Faizpur in 1912 they found themselves among a serious outbreak of cholera where three hundred had died in the town in one month yet they continued their work among the people and were able to testify that the Lord had kept them safe.

The next year they moved to Bombay to take over the work at *Beulah* while preaching in the streets and teaching women in the 'chawls', large blocks of buildings for the poor which housed ten thousand families. These ladies began a Pentecostal church and opened a school, yet were still intent on reaching out to the north of the city. Margaret and Constance worked well as a team and the ministries thrived in their hands.

The philosophy of the PMU was for the missionaries to be on the move and to get the nationals to stay and carry on the work. To a measure this happened but as these two moved on a stream of other women from the PMU came and filled the places they had vacated.

Oh The Villages!

Grace and Betty began their work in Fyzabad, south of Bombay (Mumbai) in the centre of the country. Betty learned the language while Grace, who spoke Hindustani, went out to the unevangelised villages every day. They also took the Gospel to the Melas, large Hindu religious festivals where they often encountered mobs with sticks who didn't appreciate their message. Some lady missionaries were badly beaten and had nearly died.

On one of Polhill's overseeing visits in 1914 he was able to say, 'Our sisters have a great opportunity; everywhere people will listen, though occasionally some fanatical opposer does his most to oppose the Gospel. A quiet work of healing the sick is also being done…Each of these gifted sisters has her gift. Miss Elkington is a most finished and accomplished speaker…The Lord has joined them wonderfully together'.

We leave India with a picture of these two delicate looking yet intrepid women riding round villages in a bullock cart provided by offerings from the home front and pitching their tent to tell yet more Indians of the love of Jesus. 'Oh the villages and the villages and the villages to the right and on the left,' lamented our Grace, 'how can I ever attempt to describe them?'

Bringing In Chinese

Imagine the scene. It's May 1910 and three young women are sailing down the river Thames from Tilbury docks singing 'Bringing in Chinese, bringing in Chinese, We will come rejoicing bringing in Chinese', to the tune of 'Bringing in the Sheaves'. Elizabeth Biggs, Monica Roniger and Cornelia Scharten were on their way to Yunnan Province in China having spent varying amounts of time at the Training Home.

Their journey would take them through the Mediterranean Sea and the Suez Canal, across the Indian Ocean and the South China Sea to Hong Kong. They then faced an arduous overland journey by rail, horseback, unsprung cart and sedan chair to the isolated town of Yunnan Fu to work with fellow Pentecostal missionaries Mr. Arne Kok and his wife among the unreached Tibetan tribes. They wrote home, 'China is realizing a new day. The tribes around are asking for teachers of this doctrine. A week ago over two hundred Miaos were baptised. Hundreds of others have applied for baptism... Our meetings are crowded nearly every night... numbers are peeping through the windows and hearing the message.' The success of their mission necessitated them finding a four hundred seater hall.

Virgin Fields

Hardly having time to settle in and absorb the contents of the primer *Short Cut to Western Mandarin*, Elizabeth and Cornelia travelled the three week journey north on horseback and in sedan chairs to Likiang Fu, eight thousand feet above sea level, while Monica remained in Yunnan Fu. Unlike Yunnan Fu, Likiang Fu on the Tibetan border had no missionaries and the Gospel had not yet been preached. Our PMU graduates were the first European ladies to set their feet down on this virgin field. The district had eleven tribes and was twenty travelling days in length and ten in breadth. It was an important trade centre for Tibetans so it was a strategic place to have a mission. Arne Kok had gone before them and purchased a house and later his wife and family joined this dedicated little band at the ends of the earth.

Elizabeth and Cornelia worked among the tribal women who desperately needed to understand that God loved them as women. They would say, 'We are only women, we cannot worship the heavenly Father...as women our sins are very great...' In their eyes their only hope was to be born as men in the next world.

Like their fellow Indian missionary sisters they itinerated round the villages taking Bible Women with them and took advantage of the annual fairs where all the tribes gathered for several weeks. They slept in tents and endured the rigors of the climate.

Nine Pounds A Year

Later Elizabeth and Cornelia taught in the Bible School that Arne Kok established in Likiang Fu in 1914 using their newly acquired language. In line with the PMU strategy, the emphasis was on training local workers with the aim of a self supporting church. Not only were locals familiar with the culture but whereas it cost £60 a year to keep a European it only cost £9 a year to train and keep the Chinese.

True To His Commission

In one of their first letters home they wrote, 'We praise the Lord for the privilege of going as God's messengers and with His message to the people who sit in darkness, and in the shadow of death. His angels would covet the privilege which is ours. May God keep us true to His commission'.

These ladies' dedication to the cause of the Gospel and their positive attitude was truly amazing. Writing of their first Chinese meal,

'...when we saw the peculiar food, and the dirt around us, we looked into each other's faces, and felt that we had an opportunity for victory. Then we looked to the Lord and from our hearts sang, 'Praise God from whom all blessings flow', and lifted our chopsticks and proceeded...When we are with the King for his business we can be happy under all circumstances'.

While travelling, they often slept in Chinese inns. Cornelia wrote about these 'not with the intention that her readers should pity them but to give thanks to God for protecting [them] and keeping [them] all in such perfect health'.

'The walls are as dirty as I ever could imagine. The ceilings are so old that you are afraid that they will come down... the beds are made of planks elevated from the floor about two feet, and covered with matting that is not always free from living creatures...Chickens, pigs, dogs and rats are our usual visitors of the inn'.

But perfect health gave way to sicknesses. In 1915 Elizabeth Biggs contracted small pox after one trip. Arne Kok wrote,

> 'The Lord has given to our dear sister much grace for itinerating. They often have to walk for miles and miles over rocky mountain ground, to eat day by day the plainest native food, prepared by the dirtiest hands, the sight of which alone was in former days enough to take away all appetite. They have to be content with any sleeping place, not seldom sharing their dirty smoky room with a number of other people, males as well as females. But the worst of all are these creeping visitors...*Parasitos homonios* is too fine a name for them though expressive indeed. On her last trip Miss Biggs had slept in a Min-chia home with a big heap of dirt on the floor over against her bed and a child covered with small pox in the kitchen, the only place for preparing her food'.

After Arne prayed the pox left immediately leaving practically no scars and she was fit and able to carry on as normal. In 1917, Cornelia caught typhoid and 'was near the gates of heaven' but was restored through prayer.

What happened to these ladies? Monica Roniger married Mr. Fullerton of the CIM in 1916 and they were stationed in Syemao in South Yunnan. In 1917 Elizabeth left Likiang Fu to join her sister Jessie, fresh from the Training Home, in Yunnan Fu. After a time back in England in 1920 we find Cornelia back in Yunnan in 1923.

Who Would Dare Do So?

Commenting on the bravery of these women, Arne Kok, who saw their sacrifices first hand, made a telling comment about the woman who took over from Elizabeth Biggs in Likiang Fu, yet it was a comment that applied to them all. He wrote of Miss Grace Agar after one six day journey to the north, 'For a lady alone to take such a journey, facing the opposition of a few thousand lamas, and risking attacks by numerous robber bands on the road, sleeping in the open air etc. is quite a bravery. *If it were not for the Lord's kingdom, who would dare do it?'*

The Fortunes Of The Five

Sisters Misses Maggie and Lizzie Millie (from Stirling, Scotland), Miss Ida de Vries (from Holland, 'deeply taught of God and has a loving and gentle spirit, winning the hearts of all'), Miss Fanny Jenner (from London, a qualified teacher and YWCA worker) and Miss Ethel Cook (from London and trained in business, also a YWCA worker) sailed to China and thence on to Yunnan in 1914 not knowing what lay in store for them. Bouncy letters followed telling of the villages, the tribes, the scenery, the language learning and generally the work they had been trained to do by Mrs. Crisp.

Whether there was a whirlwind romance in China or more had gone on in Hackney than was on the curriculum is not certain. Brothers Amos Williams and Frank Trevitt from the Men's Training Home had been in China two years and were already working in Tibet's borderlands. In May there was to be a double wedding in Shanghai. Lizzie Millie was to become Mrs. Williams and her sister Maggie, Mrs. Trevitt. The two couples were then going to travel to Kansu in North West China.

A Double Tragedy

The wedding took place even though Frank had been ill. After the wedding on the long journey back he had a serious relapse following an attack of pneumonia and pleurisy and the young couple's journey came to a halt at a mission station at Sian Fu. Unable to travel, Maggie stayed with him.

While he was ill Amos visited him and then went back to Lizzie at Kansu. Two days after arriving back home in November 1915, Amos died of blood poisoning and before she could travel back to be with her sister, Lizzie contracted small pox but fortunately recovered. Meanwhile Frank was getting weaker and weaker. A double tragedy followed a double wedding.

Maggie Trevitt wrote home, 'I thought my trial was heavy, but you can imagine what sorrow and dismay filled our hearts as we received the sad, sad news of my dear sister's husband's death. I feel now my trouble is swallowed in his...Oh! It all seems so strange, we cannot understand why it has happened this way but it is one of the 'All things' to both of us'. Bravely she hung on to the scripture that *'In all things God works for the good of those who love Him and have been called according to His purpose' (Romans 8:28).*

Frank died in April 1916. Mrs. Williams and Mrs. Trevitt returned to Yunnan to be with their fellow PMU missionaries and stayed in China until they went home on furlough in 1920.

Ethel Cook worked with Fanny Jenner in the villages, visiting homes, engaged in street preaching and setting up out stations from Yunnan Fu. From time to time new ladies from the PMU joined them as the work in Yunnan expanded. In 1918, Fanny Jenner became Mrs. Boyd. The fortunes of Ida de Vries remain a question mark.

Polhill's call had rung out, 'This is Yunnan's opportunity. The province is open to us now...Where are our women?' Many heard and responded to the call.

The Jesus Hall

The three Beruldsens, John, Christina and Thyra, sailed to China in September 1910 to work at the Scandinavian Tsili Mission in Suan-Hwa-Fu, a town of sixty thousand inhabitants in North China. We've already had a glimpse of their grand send off at Waterloo Station when we looked at the life of their mother Christina Beruldsen in chapter seven.

Like the other missionary ladies in China, the Beruldsen girls set themselves to learn the language while working in the street chapel called *Jesus Hall*. They started a school, visited homes with Bible Women and gave Bible studies. Interestingly they commented, 'Our main object getting the girls here is not to educate them; we want them for Jesus'.

In 1911 Christina married Parley Gulbrandsen who worked with John in the villages and the following year Thyra married Percy Bristow of the PMU and together they continued working at the Tsili Mission. Thyra and Percy spent some time at her parents' home in Edinburgh between 1913 and 1915 before returning to China with little Elfreda via Siberia. Their mission had been overshadowed by the grander work of the Roman Catholics but the humble *Jesus House* began to bear fruit reaching to the outcasts and harlots of the town. In 1917 they told of being visited 'by the heavenly host' as many were filled with the Spirit. There were messages in tongues from the Chinese in perfect English and they wrote of demons being cast out of wild people who became like lambs.

The Revival Has Come

In March 1914 letters home from Christina and John told stories of a revival at the Tsili mission at Lungmenhsien. These are a few extracts which capture their excitement of what God was doing amongst them.

> 'We are praising God as never before here in China, because the revival has come. It started on the Chinese New Year, last Monday at our prayer meeting. It came so unexpectedly. The first one to receive was an old man between sixty and seventy. He was shaking and weeping and praising God... Tuesday night the evangelist, Keuh S.S. was healed of a sickness he has had for four years. The power of God fell on him and lifted him bodily off the ground...Wednesday night David came through in holy laughter. My, it was glorious! He said after that he was *Kuoi-loh-tih li-hai*, which means 'awfully happy'. He thought he was going to heaven... Thursday night David had holy laughter again, then Nang S.S., the bookseller, had it and was trying to tell us how happy he was but could hardly do it for the Holy Spirit wanting to laugh through him. About a quarter of an hour went, then Li-fu fell down on the floor under the power of God and commenced laughing. Oh, what joy! We couldn't help but praise God; and to see the others seeking, with the hunger on their faces, was really heaven upon earth...None have spoken in tongues, but surely those who came through with holy laughter must have got the baptism. David was really 'drunk in the Spirit'...We are continuing the prayer meetings every night. We have them in our own sitting room. The meetings we have had have lasted about three hours and then the people don't want to go away...Friday night Davis the bookseller came through speaking in tongues...'

Christina Gulbrandsen had been ill but was 'wonderfully blessed and quickened since the revival'. She wrote, 'We sit and look on. He does it all. The women also are touched…the homes are different'. A missionary's dream come true!

The Most Horrible Scenes

The work in China was carried out against a backdrop of revolution which made our missionary ladies seem even braver. The Boxer uprisings at the turn of the century had given way to The Republican Revolution in 1912. Missionaries were assured by the government that they would be safe but in the provinces it was difficult to keep law and order.

The political situation in Yunnan continued to be unstable with the tribes wanting independence from the Chinese. In 1914 the rebellion was only five days from Likiang Fu and coming closer when Cornelia Scharten wrote that Chinese soldiers had met the rebels and executed them, beheading them and cutting their hearts out. The bodies were then carried on poles to be eaten by dogs and eagles outside the cities. Arne Kok with his wife and child tell of the 'most horrible scenes which [they] never hope to see again'.

The revolution secured freedom of religion, at least for a time, and it was hoped that Tibet would be opened up but missionaries were only allowed into the outer regions and the centre of the country remained closed.

Mixed Marriages

The majority of those sent out by the PMU in the early days were single women. However once on the field there was a frequent mixing of the missionary gene pool. Some PMU missionaries married without permission and had their certificates revoked, perhaps that is why their names suddenly disappear from the list of missionaries printed monthly in *Confidence*. Then Polhill decided it was necessary to increase the mandatory two year waiting period before marrying to four years.

Hudson Taylor who founded the China Inland Mission, which served as a model for the PMU, said to prospective married missionaries, 'Unless you intend your wife to be a true missionary, not merely a wife, home-maker and friend, do not join us'.

The Koks were one such couple. They were from Amsterdam but passed through the London PMU Home from where they were sent out to China in 1910. Mrs. Kok took her two year old baby, Paulus, with her to the interior and travelled with her husband until they felt the need to settle in Likiang Fu for the sake of the child's education. While staying in the inns with dangers from snakes and flies they trusted the Lord for the health and safety of the family. In 1912 another Kok came into the world who bore the name Gerard Petrus *Tibetus*, which served as a constant reminder of why they were there! They even had to travel to the coast with the new baby because of the revolution. Mrs. Kok was one indeed of the true missionaries.

'Female' Men

One Chinese worker commented, 'Send us some more female men'. The ladies we have showcased were no shrinking violets but equal to the task. Polhill called it a 'work for sweat and blood' and said, 'Don't ever start to be a missionary unless you are…prepared to rough it'. Once on the field their value was undisputed.

So how did single women fare? On the field there was supposed to be equal opportunities for men and women yet overseers were usually married couples or men. Articles in *Confidence* spoke of the great need for those with 'the gift of government'. 'Large districts are calling for the Light, to which missionaries cannot be sent till there is someone to superintend'. I'm sure many of our missionary ladies were more than able to fill that role but I wonder how often they were considered.

Further Afield

Other fields were added to those in China and India and more women volunteered to 'Go'. The next field to open up was Central Africa. A 'pioneer band' of married couples and single ladies began a mission station on the borders of Congo and Rwanda at Lake Kivu in 1919. In 1922 they were joined by one of Eleanor Crisp's daughters, Audrey, who held her nursing certificate.

Mr. and Mrs. Taylor worked in Kobe, Japan and the Richardsons worked among the tribes of North Brazil. The Pentecostal missionary enterprise was just beginning. Jesus hadn't come back and the 'charismatic moment' turned into the long haul. Missionaries began to buy return tickets.

What More Shall I Say?

At 312 Azusa Street, William Seymour told his congregation, 'Now do not go from this meeting and talk about tongues, but try and get people saved'.[2] That's what these ladies in the early days of the movement did and we honour them for it.

Not just missionary tales of long ago, these are women who led the way and opened up whole areas of our world to the Gospel so that others could enter into their labours. They sowed seeds that are still bearing fruit. Women of their day – yes. Women of the British Empire – yes, but to some degree we are all affected by the prevailing cultural mood. In the first decade of the 20th century Britannia still ruled the waves and the flow of blessing we took to the world was a mixed one. Yet that aside, their lives stand as a challenge to live the Christian life with a sharp edge, an edge that comes with 'paying a price' and a life that will count for eternity.

If the eleventh chapter of *Hebrews* were being written today *verses 32-38* may read, 'And what more shall I say?...I do not have time to tell about...Lucy, Kathleen, Margaret, Constance, Grace and Betty, Monica, Elizabeth and Cornelia, Ethel, Fanny, Ida, Maggie and Lizzie...and the many other young missionary ladies who faced difficulties, disease and often death far away from home...whose weakness was turned to strength; and who became powerful in battle and routed foreign armies...the world was not worthy of them'.

---

1 Vinson Synan, *The Century of the Holy Spirit*, (Nashville: Thomas Nelson Publishers, 2001), 6

2 Eds. Murray W. Dempster, Byron D. Klaus, Douglas Petersen, *The Globalisation of Pentecostalism,* (Oxford: Regnum, 1999), 35

11

Polly Wigglesworth
A Fiery Preacher

'All that I am today, I owe under God
to my precious wife. Oh she was lovely!'

Smith Wigglesworth

Stories of the healing evangelist Smith Wigglesworth are stuff that
Christian legend is made of. For nearly half a century he exercised
a unique world wide ministry that earned him the title, 'Apostle of
Faith'.[1] Yet, when his wife died suddenly at the age of fifty two he
lamented, 'All that I am today, I owe under God to my precious wife.
Oh she was lovely!'[2] Mary Jane Wigglesworth, affectionately known
as Polly, was his partner not just in marriage but in ministry and
from her conversion in her late teens was a fiery preacher. What is
less known is that for many years it was Polly who took the lead in
their Bradford Mission and was a strong woman of God, an equal to
Smith.

The Telegraph

One day in the Autumn of 1907 the Wigglesworths had a visitor who told them that in Sunderland people were being baptised in the Holy Spirit and speaking in tongues. Being Holiness people they believed that they had already experienced the Baptism in their second blessing experience of Sanctification. Tongues speaking was considered very controversial if not demonic in many Holiness circles.

The mission they had founded in Bowland Street, Bradford was growing and God was blessing them. They were experiencing a move of the Spirit where many were being healed and there were associated manifestations such as being 'slain in the Spirit'. Their friend was persuasive. He offered to pay Smith's fare and the four days in Sunderland changed his life. Mary Boddy had laid her hands on his head in the vicarage and he had a mighty encounter with the Holy Spirit. Smith sent a telegraph back to Polly to warn her, 'I have received the Baptism in the Holy Ghost and I have spoken in Tongues'.[3] This was on Tuesday, October 28th 1907.

Cautious of his wife's response he related the story and Polly retorted, 'I want you to understand that I am as much baptised as you are and I don't speak in tongues…I have been preaching for twenty years and you have sat beside me on the platform, but on Sunday you will preach yourself and I'll see what there is in it'.[4] Although fully involved in the work he used to struggle to speak publicly and left all the preaching to her. He had to win over his wife before he could win the approval of the rest of the folk at the mission.

That's Not My Smith!

Polly had thrown down the gauntlet and the next Sunday she sat on a bench at the back of the hall. When it was the time for the message Smith walked the three steps up to the platform and as he did God gave him the passage from *Isaiah 61:1-3 (KJV) 'The Spirit of the Lord God is upon me…'* and He was. Smith preached fluently under a heavy anointing and didn't break down and weep as he had done on previous occasions. Smith himself said, 'Suddenly I felt that I had prophetic utterances which were flowing like a river by the power of the Holy Spirit'.

Polly couldn't believe what she was seeing and hearing. She shuffled up and down the bench and said in a whisper but still loud enough for those around her to hear, 'That's not my Smith, that's not my Smith[5]... Amazing, amazing... what's happened to the man!'[6]

He was indeed different. First the secretary of the mission then his son George all wanted what he had and the meeting ended in holy laughter with many in the congregation rolling around on the floor. This was just the beginning and the years that followed saw their ministry grow and develop.

The Fire Falls

It wasn't long before Polly had her own encounter with the Holy Spirit and spoke in tongues. There does not seem to be any record of her going to Sunderland but she and her husband were certainly included in the ministry circuit that was associated with that place. *Confidence* contains a number of reports from places where they ministered. Wherever they went, either as a couple or as individuals people were saved, healed and baptised in the Spirit. The partnership was to last five years.

Polly continued to preach and shortly after her Spirit Baptism they went to a Methodist chapel in Shropshire. As she was preaching people were baptised in the Spirit all over the chapel and revival broke out in that village.

In May 1908, a short report about the Bowland Street Mission appeared in *Confidence*, 'The Lord is mightily blessing us. The results are that sinners are being saved and saints are being filled with the fullness of the Holy Ghost with signs. We are realising the blessing that comes through the pleading of the blood. There is certain victory if the pleader keeps the precious blood before him. The Holy Ghost commences to plead through him. This is the commencement of signs'. Comments like this show that their emphasis was still on the experience of sanctification as a prerequisite for the full Baptism with the sign of tongues.

The Acts Of The Apostles

A year after his own Baptism at Sunderland, Smith, no doubt with Polly's help since his formal education had been sadly lacking, wrote a long letter which was printed in *Confidence* to 'bear witness to twelve months of fullness'. Life for the Wigglesworths, he wrote 'had been like living at the time of the Acts of the Apostles'.

Underneath this letter was a note from Alexander Boddy, 'We are most thankful to learn that Mr. and Mrs. Smith Wigglesworth have recently been a blessing in the following places: Penge, Mitchan and in London at 29 Sudbourne Rd, 9 Gloucester Place (W), 73 Upper Street Islington, 14 Akerman Road, Brixton and Bethel Hill'. Smith and Polly's entrance into Pentecost made them sought after for ministry and all these addresses represented Pentecostal centres in and around London. Three are worth noting. Gloucester Place was the London home of Cecil Polhill, founder of the PMU and a respected leader in the Pentecostal Movement. Upper Street housed the mission of Harry and Margaret Cantel and Akerman Road was the home of Catherine Price where she held her prayer meetings.

They were also the first to speak at Sion College, London where Cecil Polhill organised regular meetings from March 1909. After their visit Polhill wrote for *Confidence*, 'Mr. and Mrs. Smith Wigglesworth's visit was greatly blessed, their strong faith being an encouragement and stimulus and help to all'. It was recorded that around twelve received the Baptism of the Spirit.

Another story is told of a time in 1909 when they were in Lytham, Lancashire. A drunk knocked on the door of the house where they were staying asking for help. As a group of them prayed the man was thrown to the floor three times and after that it didn't take much persuasion to get him saved. After 'signing the pledge' he went home at 4.40 in the morning a changed man. During this stay a number were filled with the Spirit resulting in a Pentecostal mission being established. In 1912 Smith was able to say how 'the Lord graciously used him [while he was still single] and later he and his wife together in the saving of hundreds of souls'.

Easter Conventions

It was a feature of the Pentecostal Movement to hold annual conventions in towns and cities around the country drawing on well known speakers of the day including, as we have seen, many of the women who are featured in this book. They were times of encouragement for the fledgling bands of Pentecostal believers as well as being a platform for dissemination of Pentecostal beliefs.

Bradford was no exception and the Easter conventions began in 1909 and continued until 1924. The first convention at Bowland Street in April 1909 saw forty to fifty baptised in the Spirit. Referring to this in *Confidence* it was noted that it was led by Brother and Sister Wigglesworth...*always a team.*

The next year a report told of many baptisms in the Holy Spirit and seventeen baptisms in water. Thomas Myerscough wrote, 'The harmony of the meetings was truly 'one accord' and the love and fellowship among the brethren was a joy to my heart...it is also a great pleasure to me to record that in all the meetings there was a sense of control, and never did I see anything to offend or hurt the most sensitive seeker or onlooker'.

Smith and Polly commented on the convention in 1911, 'It was just glorious. The Lord was kind to us, gently leading us all the time. The power was so mighty that there was no need to please, or praise or do anything but wait. God blessed and filled with His Holy Spirit...'

Her methodology for infilling with the Spirit, 'Bring everything to the altar and by a definite surrender get wholly sanctified, then the temples would be ready for the incoming of the Holy Ghost'.

Educating Smith

God had obviously brought Smith and Polly together. Smith was from a poor family and he had to work for long hours from the age of six first in the fields and then in the mill. When they met he was illiterate. Later he said,

> 'She became a great help to me in my spiritual life. She was such an inspiration to holiness. She saw how ignorant I was and immediately began to teach me to read properly

and to write; unfortunately she never succeeded in teaching me to spell'.[7]

However he never read much other than the Bible. He was a rough and ready man and she took it upon herself to train her husband's character, trying to knock off the rough edges with her honesty and humour.

Smith said of his wife, 'She was the preacher and I encouraged her to do it all' but Polly tried her best to train him for the ministry. She used to announce that the next week Smith would speak. She was sure he could if he tried. He would work at it, get in the pulpit say a few words then tongue tied and weeping open the pulpit to anyone in the congregation.

Scarbro' Poll

So who was Polly and how did they meet and become such a dynamic couple? What influences had God arranged in their lives to shape their spirituality?

Mary Jane Featherstone was born in 1860 in Hull, Yorkshire into a respectable and devout Methodist family. Her father was from a wealthy family of brewers but refused any of his inheritance because he considered it tainted money yet in contrast to Smith's family they were still fairly affluent. He was a lecturer in the Temperance Movement and encouraged Polly to grow up as a principled woman who was not afraid to speak her mind. The family lived in Scarborough where her father was a tailor and Polly was fondly known as Scarbo' Poll. It's only conjecture but it may have been that her mother had stayed with relatives in Hull for her birth or the family had moved from there while Polly was young. It was not many miles down the coast from Scarborough.

When she was seventeen, her father decided she must learn a business so she was sent to work in a milliners, trimming hats. Polly found this restricting and tedious and decided to run off to Bradford to gain a measure of independence. In her naivety she first stayed at a 'house of ill repute' then accepted service in a large house. After a time in the Salvation Army, we find her at the age of twenty one working as a general domestic servant at the house of an eighty four year old lady called Grace Smith in King

Street, Bradford. Interestingly in the same census her mother filled her name in as living in Sculcoates, Hull. Maybe something had happened to her father and her mother had gone back to her family home.

Who Are These Silly People?

One Sunday Polly was out in the centre of Bradford when she heard the sound of trumpets and drums. It was the Salvation Army holding an open air Gospel meeting. The Salvation Army had only been formed a few years before and Polly thought to herself, 'Who are these silly people?'

But she was intrigued and followed them to see where they were going. Their meeting was in an old theatre which with her strong Methodist background was considered a 'den of iniquity'. But her curiosity got the better of her and she sat down in the gallery. The preacher was Tillie Smith, sister to the Salvation Army preacher Gypsy Smith. Although brought up in a religious family, Polly had never made a personal commitment to the Lord. That day the Holy Spirit convicted her of her sin and when the invitation was given she walked purposefully down to the 'penitent's bench' and knelt weeping. Leaving her for a while, Tillie Smith came alongside her and together they prayed the sinner's prayer. After Polly had prayed she jumped up and threw her gloves in the air and shouted, 'Hallelujah, it is done!' Just a few seats away, watching this whole episode was a young man called Smith.

Officer Featherstone

Polly gave her self wholeheartedly to the work of the Salvation Army. She was a born leader and an excellent preacher. General William Booth got to hear of her zeal and through Tillie was introduced to this young soldier. He was so impressed that he gave her a commission with no training. She became Officer Featherstone.

Polly was a natural at the open air meetings but had to learn to duck when onlookers would bate the Soldiers by throwing rotten fruit and eggs at them. She once got a black eye when hit by an orange. Weathering it all she became a great soulwinner and the Army served as good practical training for Polly's future work.

Smith followed her fortunes and they became friends. However at that time rules regarding relationships with the opposite sex were strict and Officers could not associate with Soldiers, although Smith never actually joined their ranks but was attracted to the Army because of their passion for souls.

Like the regular army, Salvationists were expected to obey rules and go where they were told. Wanting to nip the friendship with Smith in the bud, a Major asked her to go to Leith, Edinburgh to help at a Salvation Army work there. This was at the same time that Christina and Eilif Beruldsen were living in Leith bringing up their family and it's not beyond the bounds of possibility that the two came into contact with each other.

While in Leith she put her heart and soul into the Lord's work yet never forgot about the man she loved. Other men admired her and she was even questioned by her superiors over one Scottish Soldier who had fallen for her but she was not interested.

Polly left the Army and returned to Bradford. She didn't stop any of her ministry activities but continued preaching in Methodist churches and in the Blue Ribbon Army, a group run on similar lines to the Salvation Army, led by Elizabeth Baxter, teacher of Holiness and Healing and who was later to be a friend and colleague of Eleanor Crisp. Even having left the Army she still counted Salvationists among her friends. Wherever she spoke the Holy Spirit moved powerfully.

The Best Girl In The World

The rules of the Salvation Army had not made the wooing of Polly easy for Smith. But love triumphed and on 4th December 1882, Mary Jane Featherstone became Mrs. Wigglesworth at Bradford Parish Church. She was twenty two and Smith was twenty three. They set up home at 70 Victor Road, Manningham, Bradford.

When he had first seen her at the 'penitent's bench', his heart missed a beat and he knew she was the one he would marry. Later he said, 'It was as if the inspiration of God was on her from the very first'. In telling the story he used to say he had met the best girl in the world.

After a time working in Liverpool Smith returned to Bradford to open a plumbing business and devote all his spare time to the Army. His marriage to Polly would in due course change the direction of both their lives but in the early years he did all he could to encourage her evangelistic gifting while he set about building up the business.

In the Home

Their first child, Seth came along the year after their marriage followed by Alice the next year who was completely deaf. Over the next twelve years the Wigglesworths were blessed with three more children, Harold in 1892, Ernest in 1894 and George in 1896 who unfortunately died at the age of nineteen, two years after Polly herself died. Before they were born Smith and Polly prayed that they would all give their lives to the Lord and they did, giving themselves to various ministries. Their children were fortunate indeed seeing the Christian faith lived out so practically on a day to day basis in the home.

Given To Hospitality

Smith and Polly were not just natural parents but spiritual parents and an inspiration to so many. On top of her preaching and church work Polly managed a large household and entertained many visitors at her home. At convention times they would get home late at night and sit round the table until well after midnight. They were also very busy making sure hospitality was provided at the conventions themselves. On reporting the Easter convention in 1909 Alexander wrote, 'Much credit is due to Brother and Sister Wigglesworth for the loving way in which they provided accommodation, and their untiring zeal to meet the wants of visitors with refreshments. The Lord abundantly bless them in their work'. At convention times their daughter, Alice, used to help them out with administration.

They lived by faith when Smith was still in the plumbing business and when he decided the time had come to answer the call for ministry around the country they still lived by faith and God supplied all their needs. As the demands on Smith to travel became greater Polly stayed at home to look after the family and the mission.

Put Down The Net

In the early days of their marriage, encouraged by Polly, Smith rented a small hall in an area of Bradford where there was no church. They called it The Bowland Street Mission. Smith would take the children to the meeting and look after them while Polly preached. His gruff exterior masked a heart of compassion since tears were always near the surface when he tried to speak publicly. He used to say, 'I was no preacher myself…Her work was to put down the net, mine to land the fish. The latter is just as important as the former'.[8] So that's what they did, she sent out the Gospel message and Smith led sinners to the Lord at the altar. They both saw the importance of training young men and women and Polly gave them a chance to preach two or three times a week. They grew quickly with role models like Smith and Polly.

Polly didn't just minister at home she went to help at other missions around which were struggling. Her fire bought them to life. She preached at women's services, men's Bible classes and her favourite, the open air meetings. When young the couple were on a cycling tour of Scotland, as they were passing through one town there was an open air meeting. They stopped and she got in the circle and began preaching. She was so effective that the provost arranged a week's meetings for her and many souls were saved. Smith used to join in these open air meetings and found more of a freedom preaching there than at the mission.

Christ Is My Master

Meanwhile Smith's plumbing business grew helped by two particularly cold winters where frozen pipes kept him busy. However, his attendance at the meetings waned and he backslid. Polly's spiritual life went from strength to strength and her fiery zeal emphasized the coldness of his heart. It was a difficult two year period which began to affect their marriage. On occasions he would go white with rage and shake with an uncontrollable temper. She carried on the work at the mission and it was her faith, prayers and wisdom that helped her through this tough period.

One night she came in late from a meeting and he told her in no uncertain terms that he was the master in the house and he wouldn't tolerate her coming home so late. Without getting ruffled she replied, 'I know that you are my husband, but Christ is my master'.[9] Angered, he forcibly threw her out the back door but she just came round to the front which was unlocked. She entered the house laughing and Smith couldn't help but join in. The situation was diffused by laughter.

Gradually Smith thawed and his passion was reignited after waiting on God and fasting over a ten day period. Polly was amazed at the transformation and in her down to earth way said that he never complained about his food any more!

I Am The Lord That Healeth Thee

Smith and Polly were thrust into a ministry that included Divine Healing in the latter part of the 1880s when they were in their late twenties. It was considered a little fringe in those days.

Every week Smith used to go to Leeds to get plumbing supplies and he met up with a group who were part of a Zion work which had its origins in Dowie's Zion City, Illinois and taught Divine Healing. This was the same group that were later to send Harry Cantel and then his wife, Margaret here as missionaries. Polly must have known about them since Dowie used to correspond with Elizabeth Baxter with whom she had been associated. Dowie actually came to London in 1900, a visit that was widely publicised and he held several meetings in Clapham, Hornsey and Islington (home of the Cantels). It was at this time that Dowie himself baptised Mrs. M.J. Wigglesworth of Bradford by immersion in the name of the Father, Son and Holy Spirit.

But for some reason Smith was unsure of his wife's reaction to this group and their teaching so he kept quiet for a while. Convinced himself he began taking sick people with him and they were healed. Quick to discover what was going on under her nose she said she wanted to go herself. Polly had not been well and she was instantaneously healed and from that time on preached the truth of Divine Healing.

Then came the challenge from the people at Leeds, why take people there when the sick could be healed in Bradford as well! Then the leaders of the group went to the Keswick Convention and in a shrewd move asked Smith to take the meetings. God continued to heal the people and so from then on Polly and Smith prayed for the sick in Bradford with extraordinary results. The work grew and they placed a big banner on the wall with the words *'I am the Lord that Healeth Thee'*. He was and He did. Later Smith erected a large flag pole outside with a red flag with that text on one side and *'Christ died for our sins'* on the other. The Gospel they preached was a full salvation for body, soul and spirit.

When You Give A Banquet

Healings were a regular occurrence and there is a wonderful story which shows not just their innovative methods but their hearts. Not everyone takes the words of Jesus literally, *'When you give a banquet invite the poor, the crippled, the lame, the blind...' (Luke 14:12-14)*.

Smith and Polly sent two people around the poorer streets of the city with a loud hailer and printed invitations, inviting all the poor and needy, the sick and those in wheelchairs to come to the mission on a particular Saturday evening. There was to be a first class meal followed by entertainment. Who could resist! Probably expecting a 'music hall' show I'm sure they were surprised when the entertainment consisted of men and women giving testimony after testimony of how God had healed them. For an hour and a half the stories of healing kept coming and everyone was deeply moved. Then these surprised guests were told that they were going to be invited back the following Saturday but this time it was they who were going to provide the entertainment. Smith and Polly prayed for them and God moved in healing power. Sure enough the next Saturday they gathered together again and all those assembled were entertained by their stories.

This is authentic Christianity at its best.

No Half Measures

If Polly believed something there were no half measures or double standards. Her faith in God's desire and ability to heal was complete. The Lord was their family doctor and on many occasions she and her husband would lay hands on their children when they were sick and see them instantly healed.

Polly once asked a visiting minister what he thought of someone who preached Divine Healing yet took medicine himself. His answer was that the man didn't fully trust the Lord. She had been referring to Smith who used to take a daily dose of salts for haemorrhoids. Challenged by this he stopped and the Lord healed him.

Following this they made a pledge. They sat across the table and looked each other in the eye and said, 'From henceforth no medicine, no doctors, no drugs of any kind shall come into our house'.[10] The only exception to this was if one of them was dying and then they agreed that they would call a doctor so as not to have an inquest and be an embarrassment to outsiders. Such was her strength of character.

Then came the test. One Sunday at an open air meeting Smith had a violent pain and he said, 'It seems to me that this is my home call'. He had been suffering with appendicitis for six months and his only hope was an immediate operation but Smith was too weak. Polly was in tears and gathered the children around her. What happened next may offend certain theologies but just then a woman came to the house. She went upstairs and cast a devil out of him and he was instantly well. Smith came downstairs and asked Polly if there was any work in and off he went about his plumbing business to the doctor's amazement.

True Partners

Alexander Boddy had made the comment that Smith and Polly were 'always a team'. It was true throughout their marriage and in ministry Smith did not inhibit Polly's gifting in any way but encouraged her. She certainly didn't play second fiddle to her husband. Women preachers and leaders were common in Holiness circles and it was this understanding that they bought into early Pentecostalism.

Holiness people had developed a well defined theology for biblical equality which gave them a firm foundation for their women to minister. There were three main themes. The *Galatians 3:28* theme which they understood as functional not just spiritual equality. The Redemption theme which argued that if women were indeed under a curse, that curse had been broken by the work of Christ *(Galatians 3:13)* and the Pentecostal theme based on *Joel 2:28* and *Acts 2:17-18* which spoke of sons and *daughters* prophesying because in the last days the Spirit was now poured out on all people. In the latter part of the 19th century there was a vast body of literature promoting the ministry of women.

Both Polly and Smith had Methodism in their backgrounds. They had been involved in the Salvation Army and their mission was numbered among the one hundred and fifty groups of the Pentecostal League (as was All Saints' Sunderland). They went to the annual Keswick Conventions and kept in contact with the Zion work of Dowie through Elizabeth Baxter. All these were hugely significant influences not just on the spirituality of Smith and Polly but on their acceptance of gender inclusive ministry even before their Baptisms in the Holy Spirit with the sign of tongues.

John Wesley promoted women preachers. Catherine Booth, co-founder of the Salvation Army (a Holiness work) had written a booklet,[11] *Female Ministry, or Women's Right to Preach the Gospel* in 1859 and women reached the highest ranks. Reader and Mary Harris of the Pentecostal League wrote books and tracts championing women preachers and the women's meetings at Keswick were a showcase for prominent women speakers of the day. Dowie expected women as well as men to be leaders and speakers and Elizabeth Baxter led by example filling a six hundred seater hall, *Bethshan,* each week in London. In many nonconformist circles women were accepted de facto. That's why in the early days of Pentecostalism the Holiness influence was crucial to the freedom that woman had in the churches.

I Get So Near To Heaven

Later in life Smith said, 'My wife once said to me, 'Smith, you watch me when I'm preaching. I get so near to heaven when I'm preaching that some day I'll be off'.[12]

On January 1st 1913 Polly had been preaching at a service at Bowland Street Mission. She walked out the door and fell dead on the mission steps. She was fifty two years old and they had been married for over thirty years. She had no known disease or illness, her heart had just stopped beating. There is no settled account of what happened next. Smith was on his way to minister in Scotland. One story puts Smith on his way out the house, another places him at the railway station. The news reached him through a policeman and a doctor.

It is said that during Smith's ministry there were fourteen instances when the dead were raised. Polly lay at their home and the story varies slightly but it seems that he stood over the lifeless body and rebuked death. One version says that she opened her eyes and said, 'Smith, the Lord wants me'. Another says that her spirit came back momentarily but the Lord spoke to Smith's heart, 'This is the time I want to take her home to Myself. She is Mine…her work is done'. So Smith released her to the arms of Jesus knowing that she had got what she wanted and although filled with sadness heavenly joy filled his heart.

The columnn *Pentecostal Items* in *Confidence* (January 1913) carried the news, 'We have to record the home call of three well known Pentecostal workers. Mrs. Smith Wigglesworth died suddenly at Bradford, Yorkshire on January 1st, much lamented by her dear ones... Blessed are the dead which die in the Lord; they rest from their labours, and their works do follow them'. (The others were Minnie Abrams, the missionary at *Mukti*, and Mrs. Murray who knew some of our missionary ladies in India.) In the same issue it said, 'Brother Smith Wigglesworh asks us to convey his grateful thanks to all who have written to him in this time of bereavement. He has been deeply touched'.

For the next thirty four years Smith preached the Gospel world wide with signs and wonders and sometimes it is difficult to sort out reality from the legend. Apparently he told a friend that after the funeral, 'I went back and lay on her grave. I wanted to die there'. Smith said that God told him to leave the grave. He continued, 'I told Him that if He would give me a double portion of the Spirit – my wife's and my own – I would go and preach the Gospel'. True or not biographer, Stanley Frodisham, said from that time a new sweetness came on Polly's husband, Smith.

Honour Her For All She Has Done

From the very first she carried a fire and her fire was added to the fire that burned in Smith. They complimented each other in the true biblical sense where 'suitable helper' *ezer (Heb) (Genesis 2:20)* means no subordinate position but a relationship where mutuality called forth the best in either partner.

Polly could certainly be considered as 'The Wife of Noble Character'. Let's look at just a few verses from *Proverbs 31*.

> *'Her husband has full confidence in her...She brings him good...she sets about her work vigorously...she opens her arms to the poor and extends her hands to the needy...her husband is respected at the city gate...she speaks with wisdom and faithful instruction is on her tongue...She watches over the affairs of her household and does not eat the bread of idleness. Her children arise and call her blessed, her husband also and he praises her. Many women do noble things but you surpass them all. Charm is deceptive and beauty is fleeting but a woman who fears the Lord is to be greatly praised. Honour her for all her hands have done...'*

A strong woman, she ran wholeheartedly with what God had entrusted to her for her generation. She was baptised with the fire of the Holy Spirit and if she were able to speak to women today I believe she would tell them to recognise the gift that God had placed within them and fan it to a flame following her example.

---

1   Stanley Frodisham, *Apostle of Faith,* (Springfield: Gospel Publishing House, 1993)

2   Ibid., 17

3   Ibid., 46

4   Ibid., 46

5   Ibid., 47

6   Jack Hywel-Davies, *Baptised by Fire,* (London: Hodder and Stoughton, 1982), 71

7   Stanley Frodisham, *Apostle of Faith*, 21

8   Ibid., 22

9   Ibid., 22

10   Ibid., 24

11   Catherine Booth, *Female Ministry: A Woman's Right to Preach the Gospel,* (New York: Salvation Army, 1975 (first published London 1859))

12   Jack Hywel-Davies, *Baptised by Fire*, 92

12

Running With The Flame

'He makes His angels winds and His servants flames of fire'

Hebrews 1:7 (KJV)

Pentecostal leader Cecil Pohill once said, 'If God calls you – mind you go - get the 'glow' in you. When you get the Holy Ghost, you get the 'go' in you!' He was referring to the missionary call but it could equally be said of all the women featured in these chapters. They heard from God, got the 'glow' and it caused them to 'go'. Not all went overseas but they ran freely with the flame wherever the Spirit of God led them.

The Fire Was The Fuel

The Baptism in the Holy Spirit is analogous to a baptism of fire which not only purifies but energises and provided the momentum for a world wide burst of spiritual activity.

The fire of the Spirit was their fuel. *Leviticus 6:13* reminds us that *'the fire must be kept burning on the altar continuously; it must not go out'*. As their lives were placed on the altar of service they were making a covenant with God. A favourite scripture at that time was *'Gather My saints together unto Me; those who have made a covenant with Me by sacrifice' (Psalm 50:5 KJV)*. As large and small groups met together reaffirming their commitment to God, He reaffirmed His commitment towards them. In the liberal outpourings of the Spirit, God was saying, *'They are My people'* and their reply, *'The Lord is our God' (Zechariah 13:9)*.

An Uninterrupted Offering

God's covenant with mankind is meant to be progressive. The fire is not supposed to go out. The priests' job was to stoke the flames morning and evening. God wants an uninterrupted offering. Just suppose the fire in these women had been caught by the next generation and passed on through the 20th century instead of 'flame extinguishing literalist theology' putting out the Spirit's fire, a warning Paul gave the Thessalonian Christians *(1 Thessalonians 5:7)*.

What if new wineskins had been found to hold the new wine? What if the culture of the church had continued to be radical and not accommodated itself to the prevailing culture of the day? What if Alexander and Mary Boddy had purposefully embraced the leadership mantle of the Pentecostal Movement and steered its course through the First World War? The Christian scene would look very different and we may have broken through to the final frontier of *Galatians 3:28 'There is neither Jew nor Gentile, neither slave nor free, neither male nor female, for you are all one in Christ Jesus'*.

Buckets Of Cold Water

In the dormitory at *Mukti Mission* the matron wanted to extinguish the flames of fire she saw on the young Indian girl. Just in time she realised that what she was witnessing was akin to the story of Moses and the burning bush. There were visible flames but the girl was not burning so she didn't throw the bucket of water over her. It's debateable whether the water would have put out this supernatural fire anyhow.

May God deliver us from ever throwing buckets of cold water over women whose inner fire is propelling them to be church planters, teachers, preachers and oh so much more. Priests are still needed to tend and stoke fires lest they go out. One rendition of *Proverbs 20:27* says, *'The spirit of man is the candle of the Lord' (KJV)* and any dealings in that tender place need to be done with the attitude of Jesus of whom it was said, *'A smouldering wick He will not snuff out' (Matthew 12:20)*.

The Torch Relay

Ashes are the testimony of yesterday's fire. They have to be removed and if the fire has gone out, it has to be reignited. The origins of the Olympic flame lie in Greek myth. During the ancient Olympic games the fire was kept burning. Then at the Berlin Games of 1936 the modern torch relay was reintroduced. The reason behind this was rather sinister because the Third Reich wanted to identify themselves with past great empires and look towards the new empire they were building which they hoped would last a thousand years.

Symbols are powerful and the Olympic torch bearer represents the continuity between the old and the new. Traditionally the flame is lit in the ruins of ancient Olympia and taken round the globe before the final lap of the journey when the torch bearer holds out the flame and ignites the cauldron in the host city heralding the beginning of a new Olympics and watched by the world. Symbolism like this draws us in to feel part of the unfolding of history. What a picture! The original flame had died hundreds of years ago yet in this atmosphere of mutuality hope is again ignited.

Redeeming this picture, the flames that fuelled these women, like the ancient Olympic flame may have died but the fire giver hasn't and He wants to reignite the flames to burn in us if we are willing to be the torch bearers and bridge the gap between the generations. If we take on the challenge it is then our responsibility to keep the flame alive and to pass on the fire to the generation that follows so they can run even faster.

Renewing The Covenant

When the tribes of Israel stood together to renew the covenant in the land of their inheritance *(Joshua 24)*, Joshua recounted a brief history of God's dealings with His people and His faithfulness. It was like saying, 'This is what God had done in the past through your forefathers. God's commitment to you hasn't changed. He can do it again'. Reminding them of past events encouraged them, challenged them and quickened faith that their lives too were part of the unfolding historical drama between God and mankind.

A glimpse into the lives of our now 'remembered' women can serve that same function. It can become part of our own personal covenant renewal with God. In our historical remembering we are challenged to say, 'Lord, you did it in them, now do the same in us'.

Our Heritage Is Our Inheritance

Our history is important. We not only learn about our heritage but it reveals to us our inheritance. When the Babylonian armies sacked Jerusalem the prophet lamented, *'Our inheritance has been turned over to aliens, our homes to foreigners. We have become orphans and fatherless, our mothers like widows' (Lamentations 5:2-3 NIV).* In God they had a rich inheritance but because they hadn't given it sufficient value, they lost it. But God in His mercy restored it to them and their lament turned to laughter *(Psalm 126).*

To continue the analogy of the games, a runner runs in his lane. These women ran according to the gifting God had given them, not their gender. In reading about these ladies maybe the Holy Spirit tugged at your heart with certain truths or things they said or did. Those are the things you must run with. The flame is there for you to take hold of and claim ownership.

Every baton that was dropped is there for you to pick up again and there are enough to go round for everyone who reaches out with their hand!

These women dug their heels in and staked out a 'land', whether it was a ministry as in the case of Polly or a sphere of influence such as investing in a future generation like Eleanor Crisp or in physical 'land' such as Carrie's healing homes and magazines. A spiritual experience such as the Baptism in the Holy Spirit can be a 'land'. One thing for sure, inheritances abound and are ours for the taking. We do not have to ask for permission.

Fire In The Bones

In *2 Kings 13:21* we read an amazing story of a dead man being thrown into a cave where the prophet Elisha had been buried. When the body touched Elisha's bones, the man came to life and stood on his feet. The life of God that enabled Elisha to do miracles while he was alive was still in his bones though physically dead. What an example of resurrection life! In those bones lay a dormant inheritance.

Now lest anyone think I am making a case to exhume the bodies of these ladies and take part in some gruesome experiment, I am not! I am trying to spell out a spiritual principle that life cannot die, the purposes of God cannot die. The life of God transcends generations. In some unexplainable way the Holy Spirit can light a flame in our inmost being that says, 'Yes, I'll run with that in my generation'. I am not talking about channelling or some metaphysical process but it is an act of faith on our part partnering with the faithfulness of a covenant keeping God who keeps His promise for a thousand generations.

It Belongs To Us

The women who have featured in this book were not perfect. They were just ordinary people who had captured something of the purposes of God and they ran with it in their generation. It belonged to them. *Deuteronomy 29:29* says, *'The secret things belong to the Lord our God, but the things revealed belong to us and to our children forever…'* Once a truth of God is revealed it does not just belong to the generation that discovered it but as the above verse says, it belongs 'to our children forever'. We are the children. The truth of God whether it is revealed in a life or in the written or spoken word belongs to us and it belongs to us so we can pick it up and run with it like the runner with the Olympic torch.

The Greek word for 'revelation' is *apokalupsis*, which is made up of two words *kalupsis* and *apo*, *kalupsis* from a verb meaning to cover or veil and *apo* expressing motion away from. Thus together they convey the idea of a veil being taken away and something being uncovered and revealed.

In 1913, one Pentecostal preacher was asked, 'How long has there been a Pentecostal Movement?' He replied, 'Over nineteen hundred years'. He then explained, 'Yes, but it has been slumbering in the Word and it has to be aroused through our faith and through our prayers'.

The 20th century Pentecostal Revival introduced new theological understanding and declaration led to experience. First a few were baptised in this way. Then more and more as the blessing spread world wide. As it was taught and many testified to their own personal 'Pentecost', it became easier to receive. Donald Gee in his history of the movement, *Wind and Flame* says that baptisms in the Holy Spirit tended to become lighter and there were no prolonged tarryings'. It now belonged to the children and what they received belongs to us.

Telling The Stories

One of the key features of the early Pentecostals was 'testimony'. The Pentecostal testimony was worn like a badge of credibility. All our women had their story of how they received the Baptism in the Spirit usually told with reference to physical manifestations and in some cases an attempt to identify the language spoken. In the imagination you can see the congregations listening with bated breath, nodding in agreement with punctuations of 'Hallelujah' as this one and that one recount their experiences.

Many too had a testimony of how God had healed them of some physical ailment. It is interesting that many had been healed from significant debilitating illnesses and it was their healing that propelled them to seek God and receive the Baptism in the Spirit.

In all the conventions significant time was given to the testimony of God's blessings and deliverance. The German Pentecostals noted that, 'The chief feature of our dear English bretheren is…testifying and the advocating of the missionary cause'.

They had caught hold of something. In Jewish, Hasidic tradition it is said that telling stories of former miracles can cause similar miracles to occur. A sick person can be cured by a tale of a miraculous cure which acts as a prayer. It's like saying, 'God, I know that You performed this miracle in the past and I believe with perfect faith that You can do it again now'.

We read in *Revelation 19:10* that *'The testimony of Jesus is the spirit of prophecy'*. As we read of the stories that give testimony to the life of Jesus working one hundred years ago, the words can act as a prophetic declaration carrying the life of the Spirit to create the same today. The life and power is in the telling.

The Mantle

Going back to our friend who had more life in his dead bones than many who were considered alive, Elisha received his anointing because he stood in the prophetic line of Elijah. He was his chosen successor. Elijah demonstrated this when he took off his cloak and flung it round Elisha's shoulders one day as he was ploughing in the fields.

Before Elijah was whisked to heaven in a chariot, he asked Elisha what he wanted from him before he died. Elisha's reply was, 'Let me inherit a double portion of your spirit'. In saying this Elisha was asking to be his spiritual heir and successor who would receive the father's 'double portion' *(2 Kings 2)*. The first words Elisha uttered after his parting were, 'My father, my father'. Then in a dramatic moment with all the other prophets looking on, he picked up Elijah's cloak (which had conveniently fallen from Elijah's shoulders as he was taken to heaven) and struck the waters of the Jordan River and they parted as he crossed over. The prophets had seen Elijah perform the same miracle. Elisha had made the point, his credentials as successor were established and now he stood in the line of his spiritual father. The point for us, there is a mantle to be picked up.

Recently I caught the end of an interview on television where evangelist Reinhart Bonnke was talking about a very significant day in his life. He had finished his Bible School training in Wales and was killing an afternoon in London before going back home to Germany. He found himself outside the house of the healing evangelist George Jeffreys, who for several decades in the first part of the 20th century had an amazing ministry of signs and wonders in Britain. Taking courage he knocked on the door and the now old and fragile Jeffreys prayed for him as he knelt down. He left and the next day he heard that George Jeffreys had passed from this life.

Bonnke said of this encounter and I quote his words, 'I've caught a mantle…That day the baton and flame met and I'm still running'.

Ancient Future

In the first chapter of this book, before the lives of these women unfolded, I mentioned the verses from *Malachi 4:5-6* making the point that the turning of hearts from parents to their children and children to their parents needs to include a generational turning. For hearts to turn they need to be softened. There is no place for generational arrogance. Yes, God does say, *'Forget the former things; do not dwell on the past' (Isaiah 43:18-19)* but in embracing the 'new thing' we must not misunderstand the concept of spiritual inheritances and ignore our spiritual lineage.

A darker side of revivals is that often new moves of God are resisted by those who experienced the last move of God. The Pentecostal Movement itself was criticised in some quarters as being inspired by the devill rather than God. With that in mind how we need our hearts constantly touched by the Holy Spirit to avoid spiritual superiority.

The generational verse in Malachi which is the last verse in the Old Testament points forward to the coming of John the Baptist who was to come in *'the Spirit and power of Elijah' (Luke 1:17)*. John symbolised this turning as he stood between the old and new covenants and he also bought a message of judgement which if not heeded would bring a curse on the land. The turning of our hearts to past generations can only bring blessing. God is a God of the generations, of Abraham, Isaac and Jacob. Elisha understood this when he cried, 'Where is the God of Elijah?'

Recently the term 'ancient future' has been coined by post modern writers. It's a healthy approach which says that the wisdom for the future is found afresh in the past. We do not live in a 21st century vacuum. We need our past to tell us who we are and provide a signpost to where we are going.

So, What Is Holding Us Back?

In recent years there has been a lot of talk amongst Christians about 'unblocking and redigging the wells'. Using the metaphor of water and wells, each of these women dug a well unique to them. They reached into the river of God and drunk deeply and allowed the rivers of living water to flow from their inmost being *(John 7:38)*. Institutionalism, tradition, cultural conformity, literalist interpretation of scripture, the First World War were all boulders thrown into the wells. When Jesus didn't come back a new prophetic paradigm emerged which took away the urgency and diluted the message.

So what is holding us back today? In some cases the very same things (apart from the war). The water is still there for those willing to remove the boulders and drink. In the ancient Middle East water was scarce and if you were fortunate to have many wells on your land you were blessed indeed. A tactic of war was to fill up the wells of your enemy. Satan's tactics were and are the same, if he can stop the spiritual water flowing he has won. Isaac received an inheritance from his father Abraham. It was a tract of land with numerous wells that had made his father very wealthy but the Philistines had filled them with earth. What did Isaac do? *'Isaac reopened the wells that had been dug in the time of his father Abraham, which the Philistines had stopped up after Abraham died and he gave them the same names as his father had given them' (Genesis 26:18)*. His servants also dug their own wells. We need to be well diggers as well as well openers.

Wells are places of warfare and we shouldn't be surprised when controversy surfaces at the very place where God desires to pour out life giving water.

Let's remove the rubble, unblock the wells and give them the same names as our fathers (or mothers!)

Their Ceiling Our Floor

Last year I visited a church in Redding, California called Bethel Church. The senior pastor is Bill Johnson and they are experiencing a time of revival where healing miracles are regularly happening. One afternoon I was in a meeting in a room used by students in the School of Ministry. At the side I noticed large collages of pictures of past men and women of God. Written at the top of the collages were the words, 'Their ceiling is our floor'.

We are supposed to take over from where they left off, not start again from scratch. Their lives provided a platform and a springboard from which to go forward but sadly more often than not that has not been the case. Following the possession of their various inheritances in the land of Israel we read at the beginning of *Judges* that *'Another generation grew up, who knew neither the Lord or what He had done for Israel' (2:10)*. Then the pattern continues throughout the book where apostasy is followed by revivals under various judges. This is a pattern that has been mirrored to a lesser or greater extent in church history. Instead of building on the revivals of past generations and successes of individuals, discontinuity has hindered the generational flow. Our women were forgotten as part of this process.

Forgotten, too, because when Pentecostal histories were written in the following decades their lives were seen through the culture of the day giving these ladies secondary or invisible status compared with their male counterparts.

The Truth Will Set You Free

If we are to catch hold of the flame, run with it for our generation and pass it on burning even more brightly, then we need to do so undergirded by a sound theological base where Word and Spirit agree.

Most women are more than familiar with the verses in the Bible which seemingly bring restriction to their ministry. To you I would say, search out the truth and *'The truth will set you free' (John 8:32)*. Not too long ago Christian leaders and theologians used Bible verses to justify slavery, now no Christian would even consider that option. I once heard it said, 'The controversial of today becomes the commonplace of tomorrow,' and I agree.

Amongst these women pioneers the prophetic nature of ministry took precedent over the need to worry over more restrictive verses. A high value was placed on their 'call', 'gifting' and 'anointing', enough to justify their ministry. One male leader at the time said that a distinct call from God could overrule accepted procedure. Early Pentecostals felt they were living in exceptional times and this called for exceptional measures which included freedom for women to exercise whatever ministries God had equipped them with. Unlike many of the Holiness women that went before them, our ladies didn't develop a common body of theology that validated their ministry, probably the urgency of the times made this seem inconsequential.

Today women need to minister with confidence *because of*, not *in spite of*, a biblical foundation. God still calls and anoints women but they need to be empowered by both the Spirit and the Word. What the Spirit of God is demonstrating in a life and saying in the Word should harmonise. God is not the author of confusion and yet this is an area where one hundred years later confusion still reigns.

It's a sad fact that in some church circles a 21st century Eleanor Crisp or Mary Boddy or many other of our ladies would be disallowed from fulfilling their ministry because of their gender unless of course they went on the mission field!

Remembered Women

Forgotten women, forgotten stories, but now their stories have been told. Catherine, Mary, Margaret, Carrie, Christina, Lydia, Eleanor, Polly, Mabel, Margaret and all the Missionary Ladies have something to say to the 21st generation if we have ears to hear. They are shouting from the grandstands of heaven, 'Run, run, run with the flame, run in the race marked out for you!'

God wants a people who pursue His presence more than power and yet move powerfully in the Gifts of the Spirit. Let egos and agendas be put aside as we become 'taken up with Jesus'. Let us reach out to the lost, lonely, sick and dying providing them with a place of rest and peace (literal places if the Holy Spirit leads that way). Let us declare Jesus is the Saviour, Healer and Deliverer. Let women be among the apostles, prophets, evangelists, pastors and teachers of the church as they were one hundred years ago. Let them be church planters and pioneers of new works. We have much ground to make up. There are still unreached people in the world, many in Britain. Will anyone reading this book get the 'glow' and 'go'?

Remembered women....We honour you.

> *'Lord, I have heard of Your fame; I stand in awe of*
> *Your deeds, O Lord. Renew them in our day, in our time*
> *make them known...'*
> *Habakkuk 3:2*

Selected Bibliography

Albrecth Daniel E., *Carrie Judd Montgomery: Pioneering Contributor to Three Religious Movements,* Pneuma: Fall, 1986

Alexander Estrelda *The Women of Azusa Street,* Cleveland: The Pilgrim Press, 2005

Bartleman Frank, *Azusa Street,* Gainsville: Bridge-Logos,1980

Burgess Stanley M. & McGee Gary, *The Dictionary of Pentecostal and Charismatic Movements,* Grand Rapids: Zondervan 1998

Cartwright Desmond, *The Real Smith Wigglesworth,* Tonbridge: Sovereign World, 2000

Chilcote Paul, *John Wesley and the Women Preachers of Early Methodism,* London: Scarecrow Press, 1991, 182

Cox Harvey, *Fire From Heaven,* London: Cassell, 1996

Dayton W. Donald, *Theological Roots of Pentecostalism,* Metuchen: Hendrickson 1996

Dempster Murray W., Klaus Byron D., Petersen Douglas (Eds.), *The Globalization of Pentecostalism,* Oxford: Regnum, 1999

Frodisham Stanley, *With Signs Following,* Springfield: Gospel Publishing House, 1946

Frodisham Stanley, *Apostle of Faith,* Springfield: Gospel Publishing House, 1993

Gee Donald, *Wind and Flame,* Croydon: AOG Publishing House, 1967

Gee Donald, *These Men I Knew,* Nottingham: AOG Publishing House, 1980

Hywel-Davies Jack, *Baptised by Fire: The Story of Smith Wiggelsworth,* London: Hodder and Stoughton,1982

Kay William K., *Inside Story,* Mattersey: Mattersey Hall Publishing, 1990

Sweet Leonard, *Soul Tsunami,* Grand Rapids: Zondervan, 1999

Confidence Issues from 1908 – 1926 digitised by Revival Library, produced by Toni Cauchi and Desmond Cartwright

The *Apostolic Faith* Issues from 1906 – 1908 *Azusa Street Papers (Apostolic Faith Newspapers),* digitised by Revival Library, produced by Toni Cauchi and Desmond Cartwright

Flames of Fire 1911 – 1917 digitised by Revival Library, produced by Toni Cauchi and Desmond Cartwright